ALL ABOUT
BREAKFAST & BRUNCH

ALL ABOUT
BREAKFAST & BRUNCH

IRMA S. ROMBAUER
MARION ROMBAUER BECKER
ETHAN BECKER

PHOTOGRAPHY BY TUCKER & HOSSLER

A Dorling Kindersley Book

Dorling **DK** Kindersley

LONDON, NEW YORK, SYDNEY, DELHI, PARIS, MUNICH AND JOHANNESBURG

First published in Great Britain in 2001 by
Dorling Kindersley Limited, 80 Strand, London WC2R 0RL

Published by arrangement with the original publisher,
Scribner, an imprint of Simon & Schuster, Inc.

WELDON OWEN INC.
Chief Executive Officer: John Owen
President: Terry Newell
Chief Operating Officer: Larry Partington
Vice President, International Sales: Stuart Laurence
Publisher: Roger Shaw
Creative Director: Gaye Allen
Associate Publisher: Val Cipollone
Associate Editor: Anna Mantzaris
Consulting Editors: Judith Dunham, Norman Kolpas
Designers: Sarah Gifford, Jamie Leighton
Photo Editor: Lisa Lee
Production Director: Stephanie Sherman
Production Manager: Chris Hemesath
Production Assistant: Donita Boles
Studio Manager: Brynn Breuner
Food Stylists: Kim Konecny, Erin Quon
Cover Food Stylist: Heidi Gintner
Step-by-Step Photographer: Mike Falconer
Step-by-Step Food Stylist: Andrea Lucich

Joy of Cooking All About series was designed
and produced by Weldon Owen Inc.,
814 Montgomery Street, San Francisco,
California 94133, USA

Set in Joanna MT and Gill Sans

Reproduced by Bright Arts Singapore
Text film output by Mik Hodson Associates
Printed in Singapore by Tien Wah Press (Pte.) Ltd.

A CIP catalogue record for this book is available from
The British Library

ISBN 0 7513 3536 3

NOTE: Use either metric or imperial measurements since
conversions are not exact equivalents.

see our complete catalogue at
www.dk.com

Recipe shown on half-title page: *Beignets*, 71
Recipe shown on title page: *Eggs in Ramekins with Ratatouille*, 28

CONTENTS

FOREWORD

Even in 1931, when my Granny Rom introduced breakfast menu-planning in the first edition of Joy of Cooking, she noted, "To balance the New Englander's codfish balls and baked beans, the Southerner's grits and bacon, and the Northerner's fried cakes and doughnuts, there is the modern trend to make the first meal of the day as light as possible".

While you won't find beans or codfish here, this volume in the new All About series aims to provide a wide range of morning choices. I think you will discover that the recipes in this book reflect how little our attitudes towards breakfast and brunch have changed down through the years, whether you want a robust array of foods for a special occasion or something fresh and light to start the day.

You might notice that this collection of kitchen-tested recipes is adapted from the latest edition of the Joy of Cooking. Just as our family has done for generations, we have worked to make this version of Joy a little bit better than the last. As a result, you'll find that some notes, recipes, and techniques have been changed to improve their clarity and usefulness. Since 1931, the Joy of Cooking has constantly evolved. And now, the All About series has taken Joy to a whole new stage, as you will see from the beautiful colour photographs of finished dishes and clearly illustrated instructions for preparing and serving them. Granny Rom and Mom would have been delighted.

I'm sure you'll find All About Breakfast & Brunch to be both a useful and an enduring companion in your kitchen.

Enjoy!

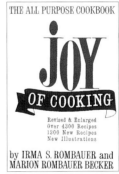

Ethan Becker pictured with his grandmother, Irma von Starkloff Rombauer (left), and his mother, Marion Rombauer Becker (right). Irma Rombauer published the first Joy of Cooking at her own expense in 1931. Marion Rombauer Becker became coauthor in 1951. Joy as it has progressed through the decades (from top left to bottom right): the 1931 edition with Marion's depiction of St Martha of Bethany, said to be the patron saint of cooking, "slaying the dragon of kitchen drudgery"; the 1943 edition; the 1951 edition; the 1962 edition; the 1975 edition; and the 1997 edition.

About Breakfast & Brunch

When you want to take the time to prepare a home-cooked meal, dinner is undoubtedly the meal you have in mind. Yet the first meal of the day – be it breakfast or brunch – can be just as rewarding to make, and it can be a satisfying and healthy way to get you ready for the tasks ahead.

At a time when so many of us seem to be working harder than ever, breakfast, especially the week-day variety, is all too often a meal of diminished importance. Even on a busy day, though, making breakfast doesn't have to be a time-consuming affair, and enjoying it need not be rushed. It really doesn't take long to brew your own cup of coffee or tea, scramble some eggs, toast bread, and cut up fresh fruit. Nor do you need much time to make a mug of hot chocolate while you reheat a muffin that you baked fresh at the weekend and stored in the freezer.

In this book, you'll find plenty of ideas that will allow you to enjoy breakfast, no matter how hectic your morning. On a weekend, you can bake not only muffins, but also delicious coffee cakes, scones, and breads, and serve them throughout the week. With a little advance planning, you can make your own cereal blends for muesli or granola and store them in a cupboard as you would purchased cereals.

Homemade fruit compotes and apple sauce keep well in the refrigerator for several days. Pancake batter can largely be prepared in advance, leaving only the final mixing to be completed before the pancakes are briefly cooked. And don't forget that cobblers and crisps baked the night before make a sublime breakfast treat.

When breakfast is delayed until late morning or midday, it becomes that charming social hour called "brunch", a hybrid of breakfast and lunch first used in England in the late nineteenth century and popularized in the United States in the 1930s. Brunch can also be an easy meal to prepare and may be served buffet style (opposite) or may more closely resemble a light lunch.

Choose your brunch menu carefully, keeping it simple. If you don't have time to do your own baking, offering bakery scones, muffins, bagels, and fancy breads is perfectly acceptable – and a good way for beginners to practice their entertaining skills. At first, you may want to avoid complicated egg dishes that might be difficult to prepare for a crowd – individual omelettes or eggs Benedict, for example. Quiche Lorraine, frittatas, and tortilla Española are popular egg-based brunch specialities, because they can be made ahead of time. Along with coffee and tea, it is customary to serve something alcoholic with brunch, such as white wine, Champagne (or the combination of Champagne and orange juice known as the Mimosa), or a jug of Bloody Marys. As you gain confidence in your entertaining skills, you can prepare more elaborate menus for a larger number of guests.

Morning Entertaining

One of the most leisurely ways to entertain is to have people over for brunch late on a weekend morning. People are relaxed, conversation flows easily, and guests linger happily at table. The menu is often easier to prepare and serve than menus offered at other times of day, making the occasion as pleasurable for hosts as it is for guests.

As at dinner, we find that the most easily managed and congenial number of guests for a morning meal is between six and eight – enough to encourage social interaction in numerous configurations but not so many that conversation turns to a din. Some occasions may call for many more guests, in which case you should follow our suggestions

for hosting a brunch buffet (below). Invite friends you think will genuinely enjoy one another, whether or not they've ever met. Invitations, whether by phone or in writing, should go out two to three weeks in advance; for a party on or near a major holiday, contact guests at least a month ahead of time, as schedules can be busy.

RULES FOR BRUNCH BUFFETS

- Buffets are a good choice for large, casual brunch get-togethers when dining-table space is limited.

- Choose a colourful, varied array of foods and display them on a handsomely appointed table.

- Make sure you have ample back-up portions of everything served, so you can replenish dishes as needed. Cater generously, for guests are apt to take larger portions at buffets.

- Label any food that isn't easily identifiable with a small card placed beside the dish.

- If you're having more than a dozen guests, set up two identical buffet lines so guests can serve themselves quickly and still have a chance to sample everything. Make sure that there is an ample supply of plates and utensils for both lines.

- If you are low on casseroles or hot plates, restrict the number of hot foods to those you can serve quickly straight from the pot or a hot serving dish, or obtain more serving vessels from a party rental company.

- Everything offered on a buffet should be easily eaten with a fork or with fingers – no knife cutting required.

Table Settings

An inviting table is as important as inviting food. Table decorations can be as natural or whimsical as you like, but make sure they don't interfere with the passing of serving dishes or block guests' views of one another – and remember that they should be suited in colour and scale to the foods served. Don't make the effects so stagy that your guests' reaction is "You went to a lot of trouble". Make them say, rather, "You had a lot of fun doing it!"

Flowers should have no detectable scent; heavy perfumes of any kind fight with the flavours of the food. Arrange flowers in small bouquets or consider floating rosebuds or other flowers in shallow bowls or custard cups. (It's a good idea to have an empty vase or two on hand in case guests bring flowers with them. Such flowers needn't go on the dining table but can be placed on a sideboard or in the living room.)

Napkins should be simply folded into quarters and then in half into rectangles or triangles. The exposed corner faces the bottom left, making it easy for the seated guests to pick up the napkin by one corner, let it drop and unfold completely, and place it on his or her lap.

Most brunches will call for just a single dinner plate to be placed at each place; for some foods, these may be heated in the kitchen (opposite) and brought to the table with food on them after guests are seated.

Salad plates may be used for the fruit courses that are often served with brunch. If you like, add small butter plates just to the left of each setting for toast, muffins, or other morning breads. Set out good-sized juice glasses, too, before the meal, positioned just above and to the right of each setting.

Practicality guides both host and guest in the setting and use of silverware. The simple rule is to work from the outside in, with as many forks as are needed placed to the left of the main-course plate and the knife to the right. If you're setting a butter plate and have butter knives, these should be placed on each butter plate in a position mimicking that of the main-course knife.

Planning Breakfast and Brunch Menus

When we think of combining dishes to make a menu, we like to recall the aphorism of the great French gastronome Brillat-Savarin: *Menu malfait, diner perdu* – "A badly made menu means a lost dinner". In planning breakfasts or brunches, simple or elaborate, first consider the season, the climate, and the probable likes and dislikes of those at table. When entertaining people whose tastes one does not know, it is a good idea to consider familiar foods that almost everyone loves.

Following are some suggested menus for breakfasts and brunches. Your tastes, circumstances, market, mood – and, we hope, imagination – will modify them considerably. To all of them add your and your guests' choice of coffee, tea, hot chocolate, or milk.

CLASSIC AMERICAN
Fresh Fruit Salad, 83
French Scrambled Eggs, 25
Sautéed Bacon, 40
Buttermilk Biscuits, 108, and honey

FRENCH FAVOURITES
Orange and Tomato Juice, 18
Savoury Cheese and Herb-Filled
    Souffléed Omelette, 32
Pommes Anna, 45

FESTIVE FARE
Bellini, 20
Onion Frittata with Sherry Vinegar
    Sauce, 33
Four-Strand Plaited Challah, 118

BRUNCH ENTERTAINING
Bloody Mary, 21
Crabcakes, 42
Basted Fried Eggs, 24
Deluxe Sunday Morning
    Coffee Cake, 110

COUNTRY STYLE
Cornmeal Waffles, 63
Chicken and Apple Sausage, 38
Old-Fashioned Lemonade, 18

FRUITY BREAKFAST
Three-Grain Apple Cinnamon
    Granola, 75
Half-Covered Berry or Peach
    Galette, 100

HEATING PLATES

Some hot breakfast and brunch dishes such as eggs, pancakes, and waffles benefit from being served on heated plates. When you plan to heat plates, use your everyday china, which might better withstand heating, checking manufacturer's information (or, sometimes, the undersides of the plates) for any precautions. If you've deemed the plates heatproof, place them on the rack in a low oven for about 15 minutes, then remove them with a potholder. The drying cycle of a dishwasher will also heat plates, or you can simply run them under hot tap water and dry them just before serving.

ABOUT
BEVERAGES

*M*ore than at any other time of day, we look to breakfast and brunch to revive and refresh ourselves. That explains why so many of us regard beverages as one of the most important considerations – when we're pressed for time, the only consideration – at a morning meal.

Coffee and tea are often in the spotlight because of the power their caffeine content has to help increase alertness. We are happy to see, however, how much attention has been paid in recent years to brewing both these morning drinks properly, using the finest coffee beans or tea leaves available and preparing them fresh, with an awareness of the finer points of preparation that bring out their best. Even if you prefer decaffeinated coffee or herbal tea, such attention to detail brings enormous benefits to your morning cup. It also does the same for even a simple glass of juice.

Sometimes, of course, beverages have the opposite goal of the everyday hot brews. Drinks like the Mimosa, 20, or the Bloody Mary, 21, aim to promote relaxation at a weekend brunch. Served responsibly and enjoyed in moderation, they can bring a most pleasurable aspect to morning entertaining.

Clockwise from left: *Cappuccino, 14; Caffè Latte, 14; Espresso, 14*

Grinding Coffee Beans and Brewing Coffee

It is essential to use the right grind of coffee for your brewing method. As a rule of thumb, the shorter the brewing time, the finer the grind must be. Espresso, which brews in 30 seconds or less, requires a very fine grind. Cafetière coffee, in which coffee grounds steep in water for a full 6 minutes, requires a very coarse grind. Propeller-blade grinders, the kind most people have, are not ideal, for they produce an uneven grind and can heat the beans, thereby releasing aromatic substances that should go into your cup and not into the air. Cool, precise tearing apart of the beans is best done in a burr mill, which has two notched blades whose position can be set for the desired fineness of grinds.

Follow the instructions given by the manufacturer for grinding times.

If you must use a propeller-blade grinder, grind the beans slightly coarser than you think you'll need, grind in 10-second bursts, and never whir the beans for more than 30 seconds, which will overheat them. Try not to grind more than 4 scoops of beans at a time. Lift the machine off the counter and shake it while it grinds. The grounds should resemble coarse-ground cornmeal for a cafetière and granulated sugar for a filter coffee maker.

The ratio of ground coffee to water is vital: the general rule is to use 1 standard coffee scoop, which holds 2 tablespoons ground coffee, for every 175ml (6floz)

water. The problem is that coffee scoops tend to vary greatly in capacity. Measure the capacity of your scoop and adjust your subsequent coffee measurements accordingly. If you prefer weaker coffee, make it at full strength and then dilute it to taste with hot water or milk.

There are a number of good ways to brew coffee, but the percolator is not one of them. Percolators violate two of the cardinal rules of good coffee brewing: they boil the coffee, encouraging bitter and sour flavours, and they pour water that is too hot over the grounds repeatedly, instead of just-right water only once.

ESPRESSO, CAPPUCCINO, AND CAFFÈ LATTE

The term *espresso* correctly refers to the brewing method, not a coffee bean or degree of roast, and it's the brewing method that gives the fullest-bodied coffee by far. Espresso machines force hot but not boiling water through finely ground coffee at high pressure. The pressure produces a syrupy body impossible to achieve by any other means and a pleasantly bittersweet flavour that lingers on the palate. The trade-off for the matchless concentration of flavour that espresso provides is that you get only a very small amount at a time. A properly brewed cup of espresso measures just 30–50ml (1–2floz), as compared with the 175ml (6floz) in a standard cup of coffee as calculated by the coffee industry. You need special equipment to make espresso – either

a moka pot for stovetop brewing or an electric pump espresso maker. Both are commonly available.

Cappuccino – named for the brown robes of Capuchin monks, whose colour it is thought to resemble – is the glory of the Italian coffee bar. True cappuccino is just espresso and steamed milk crowned by a head of satiny foam – with coffee, milk, and foam in approximately equal proportions. (Steamed milk is simply milk that has been heated with an injection of steam, usually through a tube connected to the boiler of an espresso machine.) To make cappuccino, first steam the milk (follow the manufacturer's instructions on your espresso machine or simply scald the milk in a saucepan, making certain that it does not come to a boil), aiming for a combination of milk and foam that is about

twice the volume of the milk you started with. Then brew espresso into a larger cup than usual. Using a large spoon to block the foam so that hot milk comes out of the jug first, pour no more than 125ml (4floz) milk over the waiting espresso – half steamed milk and half foam is ideal. Spread the foam gently over the top of the espresso, leaving visible a brown rim around the edge.

Caffè latte is basically an oversized cappuccino in the United States, but in Italy it is one part espresso diluted with four parts scalded or steamed milk, with no foam on top. Caffè macchiato is espresso "marked" with just a tablespoon or two of foam. In Italy, coffee with milk is considered a breakfast beverage; after lunch or dinner, Italians drink espresso.

Cocoa and Hot Chocolate

Cocoa powder, from which most hot chocolate (more correctly, hot cocoa) is made, is often sold pre-mixed with powdered milk and sugar. Because cocoa powder does not dissolve instantly in liquid but tends to form lumps that must be smoothed by vigorous stirring, commercial mixes are treated to increase solubility. You will have much better hot chocolate if you start with unsweetened cocoa powder, sweeten it to taste, and mix it with fresh milk. Some cocoa powder has been "Dutched" by the addition of an alkaline agent. Dutch processing darkens cocoa powder to a lustrous mahogany colour and helps make it more soluble, but does not necessarily improve the flavour. Try mixing with a wire whisk or rotary beater to fluff chocolate drinks just before serving and to inhibit the formation of the cream "skin" on top. Serve the hot beverage in a deep, narrow cup to retain the heat, and spoon whipped cream on top if desired.

American Hot Cocoa

250ml (8floz)

This is easily doubled.
Stir together in a small, heavy saucepan:
1 tbsp unsweetened cocoa
1 tsp sugar
Vigorously stir in, first by table-spoons and then in a slow, steady stream:
175ml (6floz) milk
Heat, stirring constantly and scraping the bottom of the pan, over medium heat just until bubbles appear at the sides. Remove from the heat and stir in:
⅛ tsp vanilla extract
Top with:
Ground nutmeg or cinnamon
Whipped cream or marshmallows

Italian Hot Cocoa

625ml (1pt)

Stir together in a medium, heavy saucepan:
60g (2oz) unsweetened cocoa
60g (2oz) cup sugar
1 tsp cornflour or arrowroot
Stir in thoroughly and set over low heat:
125ml (4floz) water
Stir in:
125ml (4floz) water
250ml (8floz) milk
Cook, stirring, over medium-low heat until the mixture is thickened and coats a spoon, about 10 minutes. Stir in:
⅛ tsp vanilla extract (optional)
Top each serving with:
Ground nutmeg or cinnamon
Whipped cream or marshmallows

French Hot Chocolate

1.5 litres (2½ pints)

A richer, sweeter beverage than cocoa.
In a medium, heavy saucepan, bring to a rolling boil:
250ml (8floz) single, whipping or double cream
Immediately remove from the heat and whisk in:
225g (8oz) plain chocolate, cut into 5-mm (¼-in) pieces
Strain the mixture through a fine-mesh sieve, pushing it through with a rubber spatula. Refrigerate the chocolate concentrate in a covered jar for up to 10 days.
For each cup of hot chocolate, stir together:
60ml (2floz) chocolate concentrate
60ml (2floz) milk, water, or coffee
Heat over low heat, or in a microwave for 45 to 60 seconds, until warm but not boiling. Stir in:
⅛ tsp vanilla extract (optional)
Top each serving with:
Ground nutmeg or cinnamon

Brewing Tea

All you need to brew tea well is hot water and the best tea you can find – and the water is almost as important as the tea. If the water that goes into your tea doesn't taste good, neither will the finished product. Don't use distilled water, for the minerals, essential for flavour, have been removed. Filtered water, on the other hand, is ideal.

Your teapot should have a wide mouth, for getting tea in and out of the pot, and a handle that stays cool. Avoid aluminium and uncoated metal, which will interact with the tea and produce off flavours. Our favourite pot contains a wide and deep inset wire mesh basket, which gives plenty of room for the tea leaves to expand and can be lifted out as soon as the tea is ready. The mesh allows easier contact between water and tea than glazed ceramic baskets, whose perforations tend to be stingy. Individual metal tea filters are also available and useful. Look for the ones that offer the most water-tea contact.

The traditional measure for tea is one teaspoon tea per cup and one for the pot, but in fact, the amount of tea should vary according to your own taste and the kind of tea you're using. The less the tea has been processed, the more you'll need. As a starting point, use the above measure for black tea, half again as much for oolong, and twice as much for green tea. Length of brewing time also should vary according to tea type – as well as whether the tea is loose or in bags. (Tea bags steep the fastest.) *Tea is not ready when its colour changes.* This is one of the most common mistakes people make in brewing tea. Tea bags should steep for at least three minutes and no more than five; oolongs, Darjeelings, and delicate black teas usually require three to four minutes; other black teas need four to five minutes; green teas should steep for only one to two minutes. Tea should never steep in hot water for longer than five minutes or it will be bitter.

Always preheat the teapot. Water for brewing most teas must be boiling hot; the exception is green tea, for which the water should be hot but not boiling (77° to 88°C/170° to 190°F). Always bring the teapot to the kettle, not vice versa, so the water will not have time to cool. To keep tea warm both during and after brewing, you may wrap the teapot in a tea cosy or thick towel. Once you've removed the leaves, tea may be transferred to a thermal carafe. (Don't use a carafe you've put coffee in, however, or your tea will take on a coffee flavour). To serve tea to a crowd, brew in advance a pot using twice as much tea as usual, then fill each cup or pot with half tea essence and half hot water as needed.

Spiced Tea

8 servings

Combine in a saucepan and bring to a boil:

95g (3½ oz) sugar
175ml (6floz) water

Remove from the heat and add:

4 strips orange zest
6 whole cloves
4 cardamom seeds, crushed
One 8-cm (3-in) cinnamon stick

Meanwhile, prepare the tea (see *Brewing Tea, opposite*), using:

3 tbsp plus 1 tsp loose black tea
1.25 litres (2¼ pints) water

Pour the hot infusion into a heavy heatproof bowl. Strain the steeped tea over the mixture and serve at once in punch cups or teacups.

Lemon Verbena (Verveine)

3 to 5 servings

This infusion method can be used for all herbal teas. The green leaves of lemon verbena have a sweet citrus fragrance.

Bring to a boil:

750ml (1½ pints) water

Remove from the heat and immediately pour over:

35g (1½ oz) dried lemon verbena (verveine) leaves

set in a strainer insert (see *Brewing Tea, opposite*) or in a teapot. Let steep for 10 to 20 minutes. Remove the insert or strain out the leaves and serve at once in teacups.

Iced Tea

8 servings

Rombauer family legend has it that this beverage originated at the St. Louis World's Fair; the circumstance, the indifference of the general public in the sweltering midwestern heat to Richard Blechynden's hot tea concession.

Prepare the tea (see *Brewing Tea, opposite*), using twice the quantity of leaves suggested. Stir, strain, and let cool to room temperature. Pour over ice cubes in tall glasses.

Serve with your choice of:

Lemon slices
Mint sprigs or bruised mint leaves
Sugar or honey
1 tsp rum per serving

WHAT TO PUT IN TEA

"Milk or lemon?" "Neither, thank you", purists will reply. But milk goes well with black tea, for its sweetness counteracts the astringency of the tannins. The old-fashioned English dictate "milk in first" or "MIF" – supposedly a sign of good breeding – was simply a way to prevent thin porcelain in typically cold English houses from cracking at the touch of hot tea. Sugar also makes black tea palatable.

Old-Fashioned Lemonade

4 servings

Chilled tea may be added to either lemonade or limeade – about 75ml (3floz) for every 225ml (8floz) of juice – for an invigorating lift. Add more or less sugar depending on the tartness of the lemon juice and your tastes.

Boil for 2 minutes:

1 litre (1¾ pints) water

135g (4½ oz) sugar

Refrigerate until cold, then stir in:

Juice of 2 to 3 medium lemons

Pour over ice cubes in tall glasses or into a jug full of ice (opposite).

Orange and Tomato Juice

4 servings

Other good juice combinations include orange and pineapple, white grape and orange, and cranberry and sweetened grapefruit.

Combine in a jug:

375ml (12floz) tomato juice

225ml (8floz) orange juice (preferably freshly squeezed)

1 tsp sugar

1 tbsp fresh lemon or lime juice

½ tsp salt

125ml (4floz) crushed ice

Fresh Pineapple Juice

3 or 4 servings

Many other varieties of fresh fruit can be turned into juice by processing in a blender or juicer. Whatever pulp remains can be removed with a slotted spoon before the juice is strained. If the juice seems too thick, dilute it with a little cold water.

Peel, core, and cut into cubes:

2 large ripe pineapples

Process in a blender or juicer, then strain the juice.

Serve it over ice with:

Mint sprigs

OLD-FASHIONED LIMEADE

In summer, when limes are less expensive than lemons – a bargain, in fact – we find new ways to use them in place of lemons in recipes such as this refreshing beverage. Prepare the recipe for Old-Fashioned Lemonade, above, substituting the juice of 4 limes for that of the lemons.

JUICING CITRUS FRUITS

Pierce the fruit with a knife and microwave for 30 seconds or place in hot water for a few minutes. Then roll under your palm on a hard surface until the inside feels soft. Both heat and pressure release juice from the cells. To quickly juice a small fruit or two, cut in half, hold the cut side of a half against the palm of your hand, and squeeze firmly. Seeds will be trapped inside. To juice several fruits, use a citrus press, which often has a built-in strainer, or a wooden reamer, which requires straining the seeds from the juice. Store citrus juice in a dark glass jar with a screw lid and keep it cold. Freshly squeezed juice retains nearly all its vitamin C for about 24 hours, although its flavour will deteriorate.

Bellini

1 serving

This luxurious cocktail was invented at Harry's Bar in Venice. For an alcohol-free Baby Bellini, replace the wine with ginger ale.

In a blender, process until smooth:

½ ripe peach, peeled and stoned

Pour into a champagne flute, then fill with:

Chilled prosecco (Italian sparkling wine), Champagne or a good Californian sparkling wine

Mimosa

1 serving

If you use freshly squeezed orange juice and a modest vintage French Champagne – or a good French, Californian, Italian, or Spanish sparkling wine – this brunch cocktail approaches true elegance.

Pour into a chilled 225ml (8 floz) champagne flute or wine glass:

50ml (2 floz) orange juice (preferably freshly squeezed)

Fill the glass with:

Chilled nonvintage French Champagne or other good-quality sparkling wine

Stir once.

Kir

1 serving

Canon Félix Kir was the mayor of Dijon, France, and a World War II Resistance hero. His favourite drink was then called vin blanc cassis, *based on the good white wine of the region and another local product – blackcurrant liqueur. Locals renamed the beverage in his honour. A Kir Royale replaces the white wine with Champagne; a Kir Cardinale uses red wine in place of white.*

Combine in a large wine glass:

175ml (6 floz) chilled Mâcon Blanc or other dry white wine

Dash of crème de cassis

Champagne Punch

20 servings

For a non-alcoholic Mock Champagne Punch, replace the brandy, rum, curaçao, and maraschino with a 750-ml bottle of cola and substitute soda water or a citrus-flavoured soft drink for the Champagne.

Peel, core, slice, crush, and place in a large bowl:

3 ripe pineapples

Cover the pineapple and juice with:

450g (1 lb) icing sugar

Let stand, covered, for 1 hour. Stir in:

½ bottle (about 375ml/12 floz) brandy

½ bottle (about 375ml/12 floz) light rum

2 jiggers (75ml/2½ floz) curaçao

2 jiggers (75ml/2½ floz) maraschino

Juice of 12 lemons

Let stand for 4 hours. Transfer to a punch bowl with:

1 block ice

Stir to blend and chill. Just before serving, pour in:

4 bottles (750 ml each) chilled Champagne

Cooked Eggnog

About 18 servings

Lightly cooking this eggnog kills any possibly dangerous bacteria in the eggs. For an alcohol-free eggnog, 2 tablespoons of vanilla extract can replace the spirits. Do not double this recipe.

Combine and set aside:

250ml (8 floz) milk

250ml (8 floz) double cream

Whisk just until blended:

12 large egg yolks

250g (9 oz) sugar

1 tsp freshly grated or ground nutmeg

Whisk in:

500ml (16 floz) milk

500ml (16 floz) double cream

Transfer the mixture to a large, heavy saucepan and place over low heat, stirring constantly, until the mixture becomes a little thicker than whipping cream (about 80°C/ 175°F). Do not overheat, or it will curdle. Remove from the heat and immediately stir in the reserved milk and cream. Pour through a strainer into a container for storage. Chill thoroughly, uncovered, then stir in:

375ml (6 floz) brandy, Cognac, dark rum, or bourbon

Cover and refrigerate for at least 3 hours or up to 3 days. Serve sprinkled with:

Freshly grated or ground nutmeg

Bloody Mary

1 serving

This cocktail is slightly less aggressive than most. For this reason it is often served at brunch. When tequila takes the place of vodka in a Bloody Mary, it becomes a Bloody María; made with gin, it is a Ruddy Mary. Replace half the tomato juice with chilled beef bouillon or consommé and you'll have a Bloody Bull; replace it all with beef bouillon and omit the celery salt and pepper, and the result is a Bullshot. A Bloody Mary without any alcohol is a Virgin Mary.

Shake well with ice:

1 jigger (40ml/1½ floz) vodka
4 jiggers (175ml/6floz) tomato juice (preferably fresh)
2 or 3 drops lemon juice
2 or 3 drops Worcestershire sauce
Drop of Tabasco sauce
Pinch of celery salt
Pinch of salt
Pinch of ground black pepper

Strain over ice in a highball glass.

Garnish with:

1 small celery stalk

ABOUT
EGGS

*T*he egg is nature's perfect shape. It is not surprising that so elegant a container should turn out to hold a small treasure of balanced nutrients – proteins, fats, vitamins, and minerals.

Though they are most commonly thought of as morning menu items, eggs and egg dishes may be acceptably served at any meal: fried, scrambled, boiled, poached, baked, or incorporated into omelettes or a soufflé. And almost unlimited variations of meat, vegetables, or fish may accompany or be folded into them.

No egg dish really succeeds, however, unless the eggs are strictly fresh and are cooked with due respect for their delicacy and sensitive response to heat. In only one type of preparation should the heat be high and brief – for omelettes, 30–31. Otherwise, dishes in which eggs predominate invariably do best if gently cooked and carefully timed.

Leek Tart, 35

Making Fried Eggs

Fried eggs are actually sautéed eggs – cooked in a small amount of fat, usually butter, but sometimes bacon fat or olive or other vegetable oil. Fried eggs, like eggs cooked other ways, will quickly turn tough and rubbery if the heat is too high. There are some cooks who like the brown, crispy edges of a fast-cooked fried egg, but a lower temperature yields a tender, more delicate egg.

If you are concerned about presentation, truly fresh eggs make the best-looking fried eggs, with their neat, compact shape and high, well-centred yolk. Using a non-stick frying pan makes it easier to slide the cooked eggs onto a plate. If you do not have a non-stick frying pan, be sure to use enough butter or other fat to generously coat the bottom of the pan.

> ### BASTED FRIED EGGS
> For sunny-side-up eggs that are more cooked on top, cook the eggs in 30 to 45g (1 to 1½ oz) fat. Collect the hot fat from the edges of the pan and dribble it over the eggs. Baste in this manner 2 or 3 times, covering the pan between bastings.

Eggs Beatrice

4 servings

Heat in a large frying pan over medium heat:

30g (1oz) butter

Add and cook until heated through:

4 large tomato slices, 6mm to 1cm (¼ to ½ in) thick

Remove from the pan and place 1 slice on each of:

4 English muffin halves, toasted, or 4 *Golden Potato Pancakes*, 45, each about 8cm (3in) in diameter

Quickly wipe out the pan with a paper towel. Add:

15g (½ oz) butter

When the butter is foaming, break into the pan:

4 eggs

Season with:

Scant ⅛ teaspoon salt
Pinch of ground black pepper

Cover and cook until the whites are completely set and the yolks are just barely beginning to thicken around the edges, 4 to 6 minutes. Place the eggs on top of the tomatoes. Increase the heat to high and add to the pan:

30g (1oz) butter
1 tbsp finely chopped shallots or spring onions
3 tbsp red wine vinegar

Boil the mixture until slightly reduced. Stir in:

2 tbsp chopped mixed fresh herbs, such as parsley, tarragon, and chives

Taste and adjust the seasonings. Pour the sauce over the eggs and serve.

Egg in a Hole

1 or 2 servings

Young eaters get a kick out of this dish. Using a 6.5-cm (2½-in) biscuit cutter or small glass, cut a round hole out of the centre of:

2 slices sandwich bread

Melt in a large frying pan over medium heat:

30g (1oz) butter

Add the bread slices and cook for about 30 seconds. Crack into the holes:

2 eggs

Do not worry if some of the white remains on top of the bread. Add more butter if needed. When the egg begins to set, 2 to 3 minutes, flip the bread and egg using a spatula. Fry the other side until the eggs are done to your liking. Serve on a warmed plate. Fry the leftover rounds of bread and serve them as well.

> ### EGG SIZES
> Although the most common egg size sold today is medium, any size may be used for preparations such as fried, boiled, or poached – that is, when the size of the egg has no effect on the overall recipe. Otherwise, our recipes state when large eggs should be used. The typical serving is 1 or 2 eggs per person.

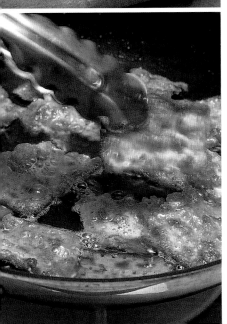

French Scrambled Eggs

2 servings

It takes both patience and a bit of technique to make great looking and tasting scrambled eggs. First, beat the eggs until the whites and yolks are completely blended. The addition of cream, butter, milk, or even water will keep the eggs more tender when cooked to medium doneness. But the liquid can also separate out and turn the eggs watery, especially if they are cooked too quickly – gentle heat is essential for producing soft, delectable eggs. The lower the heat, the longer it takes the eggs to cook, and the creamier the result. The French technique takes this principle to an extreme by cooking scrambled eggs in a double boiler. Infrequent stirring will produce large, uneven curds; more constant, careful stirring and scraping of the bottom of the pan will result in more delicate, billowy curds and creamier eggs. Vigorous stirring will produce small curds. Finally, scrambled eggs must be served immediately. We recommend transferring them to warmed plates while they are still slightly underdone. They will continue to cook and firm up on their way to the table.

Melt in the top of a double boiler over – not in – boiling water:

15g (½ oz) butter

Beat together until the whites and yolks are completely combined:

3 to 4 eggs

30g (1oz) butter, cut into small pieces

¼ tsp salt

⅛ tsp ground black pepper

Pour the eggs into the double boiler and stir with a wooden spoon as the butter melts. Continue stirring, scraping the bottom and sides of the pan, until the eggs have thickened into soft, creamy curds, 10 to 15 minutes. Serve immediately.

Matzo Brei

1 serving

For centuries when Passover came, Jewish cooks around the world invented different ways to use matzo, unleavened bread. This recipe for matzo and eggs can compete with any brunch pancakes or waffles.

For each person use:

2 unsalted matzos

1 large egg, well beaten

Hold the matzos under hot running water to quickly wet both sides without making them soggy. Place in a colander to drain. Tear the matzos into 6- to 8-cm (2½- to 3-in) pieces and set in a bowl. Add the egg and gently stir to coat the matzo pieces. Season to taste with:

Salt

Heat in a large frying pan:

3mm (⅛ in) vegetable oil or chicken fat

Spread the matzo mixture in the pan in a very thin layer, spreading it with a large spoon or spatula. Cook, turning the pieces as they brown, until medium-brown and crispy. If making a large quantity for a crowd, use 2 pans and keep the cooked matzo brei warm in a 93°C (200°F) Gas ¼ oven. Serve warm, passing the salt shaker or a combination of sugar and cinnamon.

Eggs Benedict

2 to 4 servings

This enduring brunch speciality (opposite) was apparently invented at the famed Delmonico's restaurant in New York City in the 1920s. Then, as now, hollandaise sauce was considered essential. The basic construction lends itself to improvisation. In place of ham or bacon, the eggs can be placed on top of smoked salmon, fried tomatoes, or artichoke bottoms and set upon a base of thick-cut toast, corn bread, or potato pancakes. The eggs can even be fried or medium-boiled and carefully peeled instead of poached.

Place on warmed plates or a warmed serving platter:

2 English muffins, split, toasted, and buttered

Arrange on the muffins:

4 thick slices ham or cooked bacon, warmed

Set on each slice of ham one of:

4 *Poached Eggs, right,* well drained

Divide among the 4 eggs to coat:

125ml (4floz) *Blender Hollandaise Sauce, opposite*

Serve immediately, passing extra sauce on the side if desired.

Eggs with Smoked Salmon

4 servings

Place on warmed plates or a warmed serving platter:

4 slices light rye or pumpernickel bread, toasted and buttered

Arrange on the toast:

4 thin slices smoked salmon

Set on each slice of salmon one of:

4 *Poached Eggs, right,* well drained

Divide among the 4 eggs to coat:

125ml (4floz) *Scandinavian Mustard-Dill Sauce, below,* or *Blender Hollandaise Sauce, opposite*

Sprinkle with:

Snipped fresh dill

Serve immediately, passing extra sauce on the side if desired.

Scandinavian Mustard-Dill Sauce

About 250ml (9floz)

Whisk together in a medium bowl until smooth:

3 tablespoons Swedish or Dijon mustard

2 tablespoons snipped fresh dill

1 to 2 tablespoons sugar

2 tablespoons fresh lemon juice or red wine vinegar, or to taste

Salt and ground black pepper to taste

Pinch of ground cardamom

Gradually add, whisking constantly, until blended and smooth:

125ml (4floz) vegetable oil

Cover and let stand for 2 to 3 hours before serving to allow the flavours to develop. Serve at room temperature or chilled. This sauce will keep, covered and refrigerated, for up to 2 days.

Poached Eggs

4 servings

Poached eggs should be poached, not simmered or boiled. Start with fresh eggs cracked just before cooking. While water is certainly the most common medium for poaching eggs, other liquids, including stock, wine, cream, milk, or sauce, can be used. The eggs can be poached ahead of time and refrigerated for up to 24 hours; transfer to a bowl of iced water the moment they are done, then, when ready to serve, carefully transfer to a large bowl full of 65°C (150°F) water, cover, and let stand for 15 minutes.

Heat 5 to 8cm (2 to 3in) of water in a large saucepan over medium heat until almost boiling. Add:

1 tbsp vinegar (any type)

Crack into 4 small cups and slide one by one from the cup into the simmering water:

4 eggs

If an egg sinks to the bottom, wait until it is nearly set before trying to dislodge it with a slotted spoon so the yolk does not break. Keep the water just below a simmer, reducing the heat to low if necessary. Cook until the whites are set and the centres are still soft. Remove with a large slotted spoon and set in a second pan of water warmed to 65°C (150°F). Cover and stand for 15 minutes; reheat if the temperature falls below 63°C (145°F). Drain each egg with a slotted spoon and hold it against a clean, dry tea towel to absorb as much water as possible. If desired, use scissors to trim away any ragged edges.

CLARIFIED BUTTER

Butterfat that has been separated from its water and milk keeps about three times longer, does not burn in sautéing, and has a pure clean flavour. Cut unsalted butter into small pieces and melt over low heat without stirring and without allowing the butter to sizzle, then simmer for 10 to 15 minutes. Strain the mixture well and let the clear yellow liquid cool before covering. When chilled, clarified butter becomes grainy. It should be used only in cooking.

Blender Hollandaise Sauce

About 250ml (9floz)

The clarified butter should be very warm, since the sauce is not reheated. Place in a blender or food processor:

3 large egg yolks

2 tsp fresh lemon juice, or to taste

Ground white pepper or hot red pepper sauce to taste

Salt to taste

Process on high speed for 1 minute. With the machine running, add in a slow, steady stream:

125ml (4floz) very warm to hot *Clarified Butter*, left

By the time all the butter is poured in – about 1 minute – the sauce should be thickened. If not, process on high speed for about 20 seconds more. Taste and adjust the seasonings. Serve immediately or keep warm by submerging the blender container in warm (not hot) water. Serve warm.

Making Baked Eggs

There are several advantages to baking eggs. First, the heat of the oven cooks eggs slowly and evenly, eliminating many of the challenges of stove-top cooking. Next, it is both convenient and attractive to serve eggs in the little ramekins, gratin dishes, or casseroles in which they were baked (the French call this presentation *en cocotte*). Finally, this method is wonderfully flexible. Classically speaking, baked, or shirred, eggs are cooked in buttered moulds with nothing more than salt and pepper and a little butter or cream. Sautéed vegetables, cooked breakfast meats, or smoked fish can be added to the moulds, or the eggs can be topped with cheese or sauces of various kinds. (If you wish to cut back on fat, eliminate the butter or cream and simply cover each dish to trap the steam and prevent the surface from drying out.)

125-ml (4-floz) ramekins, which hold one egg, are commonly used, but you can use something larger – 175-ml (6-floz) custard cups, oven-proof coffee cups, dessert bowls, or large muffin tins. Baked eggs should be cooked until the whites are set and the yolks just beginning to set. Care should be taken not to overcook the eggs: the ramekins will retain heat and continue to cook them after they are removed from the oven.

Baked Eggs

1 serving

To bake 2 eggs, use a 175-ml (6-floz) ramekin, double all other ingredients, and bake for about 18 minutes.

Preheat the oven to 180°C (350°F) Gas 4. Lightly butter a 125-ml (4-floz) ramekin and sprinkle it with:

Pinch of salt
Pinch of ground black pepper
Crack into it:
1 egg
Drizzle over the top:

1 tsp to 1 tbsp whipping or double cream
½ tsp melted butter (optional)
If you do not use cream or butter, loosely cover the top of the ramekin with foil. Bake in a water bath until the white is firm and the yolk is thickened, about 15 minutes. Serve directly from the ramekin with buttered toast.

MAKING A WATER BATH
Choose a roasting tin large enough to accommodate the moulds without them touching one another, and line it with a tea towel. Slide the ramekin-filled tin into the preheated oven, and immediately pour in enough hot water to come one-half to two-thirds up the sides of the ramekins.

Eggs in Ramekins with Ratatouille

6 servings

Have ready:
375ml (12floz) *Ratatouille*, 49
Preheat oven to 200°F (400°F) Gas 6. Lightly grease 12 ramekins, about 3.8cm (1½ in) deep and 7.5cm (3in) in diameter with:
45g (1½ oz) butter
Sprinkle the bottoms with:
Salt and ground black pepper
Spoon an equal portion of the ratatouille into each ramekin, reserving a small portion for use as garnish. Cover to keep warm. Using a total of:
12 eggs
break 1 egg into each ramekin and sprinkle lightly with:
Salt and ground black pepper
Arrange the ramekins in a baking dish and pour boiling water around them. Bake until the whites are firm and the yolks are runny or just starting to set, 10 to 12 minutes. Spoon a little of the reserved ratatouille on top of each serving (opposite). Serve 2 to each guest along with:
French bread or buttered toast
Cover a small plate with a napkin, and place the ramekins on the napkin. Provide each guest with a salad fork and a small spoon.

Making Omelettes

There are three basic types: rolled, flat, and souffléed. All are made from beaten eggs cooked so that the exterior is firm and smooth while the inside is somewhere between runny and barely moist. Unlike most egg dishes, omelettes are cooked over high heat. The classic omelette, a French omelette, is rolled or folded, typically around a savoury filling. The flat omelette is made much like a large pancake. Souffléed omelettes are made puffy and light by separating the eggs and beating the egg whites until airy and light.

In making omelettes, the right pan makes an enormous difference. Purists insist on a special heavy-gauge omelette pan, used solely for omelette making and never washed – it is simply rubbed with a soft cloth and a handful of salt. While these pans do produce superior omelettes, not many of us have the luxury of a kitchen stocked with single-purpose equipment. In truth, any slope-sided, heavy-based pan with a smooth surface will do. Non-stick pans allow you to reduce the amount of cooking fat.

An omelette is easiest to manage and looks best prepared in the proper size pan. For a 2-egg omelette, a pan with a 15- to 20-cm (6- to 8-in) diameter is best. A 3- to 5-egg omelette needs a 20- to 23-cm (8- to 9-in) pan, and if you are showing off with a 6- to 8-egg omelette, wield a 25- to 30-cm (10- to 12-in) pan. Small is beautiful for French omelettes: cutting a large rolled omelette into many servings can result in a sloppy mess. If you do want to attempt a large omelette, try a flat omelette or frittata, 33.

HOW TO MAKE A FRENCH OR ROLLED OMELETTE

A perfectly executed omelette requires a certain practiced rhythm. The eggs should be beaten only enough to thoroughly blend the whites and yolks, not enough to incorporate air or make them frothy.

1 Add the eggs to the hot pan the moment the butter's bubbling begins to subside but before it starts to brown. Grasp the handle of the pan and shake the eggs back and forth while stirring the eggs with your other hand. The best tool for stirring is a table fork, held flat so it does not touch the pan bottom. In as little as 20 to 30 seconds, the eggs will begin to form curds and set firmly along the bottom, while the surface will remain moist. This is your cue to stop stirring and, with the back of the fork, shape the omelette into a neat circle by gently spreading the eggs evenly around the pan. With the surface still moist, quickly add any filling you might want.

2 Roll the omelette with what can be described as a soft fold. Tilt the pan away from you at about a 45-degree angle and use the fork to coax the top third of the omelette away from the handle and down over onto itself (and the filling if there is one). If you prefer an omelette with a lightly browned surface, let the omelette sit for a few seconds on the burner.

3 With a warm plate waiting, slant the pan to 90 degrees or more. Make a second fold by sliding the omelette out of the pan until it falls seam side down on the plate. Straighten the edges of the omelette to form a neat oval and serve immediately.

French Omelette

1 serving

The success of any omelette demands that the fat in the pan be hot enough to gently set the exterior of the omelette at once, but not so hot as to toughen it before the rest of the egg cooks. With the pan at the proper heat, a 2-egg omelette takes less than 1½ minutes to cook from the time the beaten egg hits the hot pan until the finished omelette is rolled out onto a warmed plate. Have all your ingredients ready when you start cooking. When making more than one omelette, beat the total number of eggs, and use a ladle or measuring cup to pour 60ml (2fl oz), for each 2-egg omelette. Keep melted butter and filling ingredients by the stove and move quickly, making the omelettes one by one. Serve them as they are ready, or keep them warm in a 93°C (200°F) Gas ¼ oven and serve when all are finished. If making more than four, use another pan or two. Attention to more than one pan at a time is a skill that needs to be developed. Stagger the different pans' "schedules" so that the omelettes are not all at the same stage at once.

Combine and beat with a fork until the whites and yolks are blended:

2 large eggs
Scant ⅛ tsp salt
Pinch of ground black pepper

Melt in a 15- to 20-cm (6- to 8-in) frying pan over medium-high heat:

15g (½ oz) butter

Tilt the pan to coat the sides and bottom thoroughly. When the butter is hot and the foam has subsided, pour in the eggs. Shake the pan back and forth while stirring the eggs with your other hand, using a fork held flat, just above the pan bottom. If adding a filling, do so once the bottom has set, placing it in a line in the centre of the omelette. Use the fork to begin to roll the edge of the omelette towards the centre, all the while tilting the pan to fold the omelette against the pan wall. Check if the underside of the omelette is as browned as you wish. If not, leave on the heat for a few seconds more before serving. With a warmed plate at the ready, tilt the pan up until the omelette makes a second fold and slips seam side down onto the plate.

FILLING OMELETTES

An omelette's filling should complement the delicate flavour of the eggs, not overwhelm it. The classic French omelette is sometimes made with only eggs and salt and pepper; ingredients such as chopped herbs and finely diced meats may be added directly to the beaten eggs, while more substantial fillings may be placed in the middle of the omelette just before it is rolled up. To fill a 2-egg omelette, have ready 80 to 125ml (3 to 4fl oz) of filling. Place 2 tablespoons in the omelette while it is still in the pan and before you have rolled it, along the middle third. Reserve the remainder for a final garnish on top. Or fold the omelette without a filling and then, after it is on the plate, cut an incision along the top and fill it with the warm garnish. Fillings should be fully cooked (if cooking is necessary at all) and neither too cold nor too hot when added to an omelette.

FOLDED OMELETTE

1 serving

For a beginner, the firmer texture of this omelette is a bit more manageable. It is neatly folded in half and does not require the tricky shaking and stirring action of the French omelette.

Prepare *French Omelette, left,* using 2 eggs and adding 2 tablespoons milk, cream, or stock to the beaten eggs. As the omelette cooks, instead of stirring and shaking the pan, lift the edges of the omelette with a pancake turner and tilt the frying pan to allow the uncooked egg mixture to run to the bottom. When all is an even consistency, place any filling on the bottom half and fold the omelette in half, forming a half-moon shape. Serve immediately on a warmed plate.

EGG-WHITE OMELETTE

1 serving

For anyone on a low-cholesterol, reduced-fat diet, it is possible to modify egg recipes to eliminate the yolks. Since the yolks carry the richness and flavour of the egg, we recommend compensating by adding more in the way of your favourite seasonings and fillings.

Prepare *Folded Omelette, above,* substituting 3 egg whites for the 2 whole eggs, eliminating the milk, cream, or stock, and using vegetable oil in place of butter. Add chopped herbs and plenty of seasonings to the whites before adding them to the pan. Choose a moist, zesty filling.

Savoury Cheese and Herb-Filled Souffléed Omelette

4 servings

This impressive creation is made by separating eggs and beating the whites until stiff, as you would for a soufflé. The omelette is then cooked in an omelette pan until puffy and light and can be either left flat or folded over to envelop a filling. We especially like sweet fillings, such as fruit or preserves, with these omelettes, but savoury cheese or herb fillings can also be delicious. Whatever your choice, do not overdo it. Use no more than 5 tablespoons prepared fruit or a few tablespoons of jam thinned with a teaspoon of liquor for 4 eggs. A properly executed souffléed omelette has a lovely brown, firm, dry exterior enveloping a soft, creamy, airy centre. With the added volume of the beaten whites, you get more servings from fewer eggs, and 1 egg per person satisfies most appetites.

Preheat the oven to 190°C (375°F) Gas 5.

Combine and whisk until thick and light:

4 large egg yolks

Salt and ground black pepper to taste

In a separate bowl, beat until stiff but not dry:

4 large egg whites

Pinch of salt

Fold the yolk mixture gently into the whites. Melt in a 25-cm (10-in) oven-proof frying pan over medium heat:

15 to 30g (½ to 1oz) butter

When the foam has subsided, pour the batter into the pan, spread evenly, and smooth the top. Shake the pan after a few seconds to discourage sticking and then cover the pan with a lid whose underside has been buttered to prevent sticking. Reduce the heat and cook for about 5 minutes. Remove the cover and sprinkle the top of the omelette with:

2 tbsp chopped herbs (chives, parsley, chervil, or a combination)

4 tbsp grated cheese

Place the pan in the oven until the top is set, 3 to 5 minutes. Either fold the omelette in half or slide it out onto a warmed plate and serve with:

Tomato sauce or *Salsa Verde Cruda*, 49

Tortilla Española (Potato Omelette)

6 servings

In some places, a Spanish omelette is a rolled one filled with peppers and tomatoes – but this authentic Spanish version is flat (but usually thick) and filled with potatoes and onions. Tortilla means "little cake" but in this case has nothing to do with the little cakes of corn or wheat flour called tortillas in Mexico and Central America.

Heat in a large frying pan over medium heat:

2 tbsp olive oil

Add:

1 large onion (about 225g/8 oz), cut into slices 3-mm (⅛-in) thick

Salt and ground black pepper to taste

Cook until the onions are soft and golden, reducing the heat as they cook, about 20 minutes. Remove to a large bowl. Heat in the same pan over high heat:

60ml (2floz) olive oil

Add:

450g (1lb) red-skinned potatoes, peeled and cut into slices 3-mm (⅛-in) thick

Cook until golden brown, 10 to 12 minutes. Reduce the heat to medium-high if the oil gets too hot and smoky. Toss the potatoes often with a metal spatula, separating most of the slices that stick together. Remove the potatoes with a slotted spoon to paper towels to drain. Set aside the pan with the oil in it. Add to the onions and mix together:

6 large eggs

½ tsp salt

Ground black pepper to taste

Sprinkle the potatoes with:

Salt and ground black pepper to taste

Add the potatoes to the egg mixture and toss to coat the slices well with the eggs. Return the pan to high heat to heat the remaining oil in the pan. When hot, add the egg mixture and immediately reduce the heat to low. Let the omelette cook for 3 to 4 minutes, undisturbed, until the bottom is golden and the eggs are two-thirds to three-quarters set. Shake the pan from time to time to make sure the omelette does not stick. If it does, slide a metal spatula under the omelette to free it from the pan and continue cooking. Place a lightly oiled large heatproof plate upside down over the omelette and flip the pan to turn the omelette over. Slide the omelette back into the pan to cook the second side. Cook until golden and set, 2 to 3 minutes more. Shake the omelette loose from the pan and slide onto a clean plate. Cut into 6 wedges and serve hot or at room temperature.

Onion Frittata with Sherry Vinegar Sauce

4 to 6 servings

In flat omelettes, eggs assume a supporting role, binding the ingredients and adding richness while the emphasis is on the filling. A flat omelette can be thick or thin, but it is always too hearty and awkward to roll or fold; instead, it is served in wedges, much like an open-faced pizza. Flat omelettes can be made ahead and served at room temperature.

Caramelize, 46:

700g (1½ lb) onions

Just before removing from the heat, season with:

1 tbsp sherry vinegar

Plenty of ground black pepper

Preheat the grill.

Beat with a fork just to combine:

5 large eggs

½ tsp salt

2 tbsp chopped fresh parsley

Stir in the onions. Melt in a medium, ovenproof, non-stick frying pan over medium heat:

15g (½ oz) butter

When the butter foams, swirl it around the pan, then pour in the eggs. Shake the pan back and forth a few times to loosen the bottom, then turn the heat down to medium-low, cover, and cook until the eggs are set and well coloured on the bottom, about 10 minutes. Uncover and place under the grill. When the frittata is set and nicely browned on top, slide it onto a serving plate. Return the pan to medium heat.

Add:

15g (½ oz) butter

When the butter foams, pour in:

1 tbsp sherry vinegar

Rapidly shake the pan back and forth to combine.

Spoon the sauce over the eggs, then serve.

Quiche Lorraine

One 23-cm (9-in) quiche; 4 to 6 servings

This brunch and lunch classic is a speciality of the Lorraine region of northeastern France, where it was first made as early as the sixteenth century. Traditional quiche Lorraine contains no cheese.

Prepare:

Short Crust Pastry Dough, below

Roll out the dough and fit it into a 23-cm (9-in) loose-based tart tin. Refrigerate the pastry for at least 30 minutes.

Position the rack in the lower third of the oven. Preheat the oven to 200°C (400°F) Gas 6.

Smooth a sheet of foil, shiny side down, over the bottom and sides of the pastry, flaring the excess foil, like an awning, over the pastry edge to keep it from overbrowning. Fill the liner with raw beans, rice, or baking beans, banking the weights against the sides of the pastry if you do not have enough to fill the case to the brim. Bake the pastry for 20 minutes with the weights in place to set the pastry. Carefully lift out the foil with the weights inside. Prick the pastry thoroughly with a fork, return it to the oven and bake until the pastry is golden brown all over, 5 to 10 minutes more. Check the pastry periodically; if it puffs along the bottom, prick it with a fork, then press down gently with the back of a spoon. Whisk together, then brush the inside with:

1 large egg yolk
Pinch of salt

Return to the oven until the egg glaze sets, 1 to 2 minutes. Reduce the oven temperature to 190°C (375°F) Gas 5.

Cook in a heavy frying pan over medium heat, stirring constantly, until the fat is almost rendered but the bacon is not yet crisp:

115g (4 oz) sliced bacon, cut into 2.5-cm (1-in) pieces

Drain on paper towels. Beat together:

3 large eggs, lightly beaten
375ml (12 floz) crème fraîche or whipping or single cream
½ tsp salt
¼ tsp ground black pepper
Pinch of freshly grated or ground nutmeg

Arrange the bacon on the bottom of the pastry and pour the custard into it. Bake until the filling is browned and set, 25 to 35 minutes.

Short Crust Pastry Dough

One 23-cm (9-in) pie shell

Using a rubber spatula, thoroughly mix in a large bowl:

180g (6oz) plain flour
½ tsp white sugar, or 1½ tsp icing sugar
½ tsp salt

Add:

180g (6oz) solid vegetable oil, or 90g (3oz) solid oil and 60g (2oz) cold unsalted butter

Break the fat into large chunks; if using butter, cut into small pieces, then add to the flour mixture. Cut the fat into the dry ingredients by chopping vigorously with a pastry blender or by cutting in with 2 knives. Periodically stir dry flour up from the bottom of the bowl and scrape clinging fat off the pastry blender or knives. Some of the fat should remain in pea-sized pieces; the rest should be reduced to the consistency of coarse crumbs. The mixture should seem dry and powdery, not pasty or greasy. Drizzle over the flour and fat mixture:

3 tbsp iced water

Using the rubber spatula, cut with the blade side until the mixture looks evenly moistened and begins to form small balls. Press down on the dough with the flat side of the spatula. If the balls of dough stick together, you have added enough water; if they do not, drizzle over the top:

1 tbsp iced water

Cut in the water, again using the blade of the spatula, then press with your hands until the dough coheres. The dough should look rough, not smooth. Press the dough into a round flat disk and wrap tightly in cling film. Refrigerate for at least 30 minutes – preferably for several hours – for up to 2 days before rolling. The dough can also be wrapped airtight and frozen for up to 6 months; thaw completely before rolling.

Leek Tart (Flamiche aux Poireaux)

One 23-cm (9-in) tart; 6 servings

This is a rich leek and cream pie from northern France.

Prepare:

Short Crust Pastry Dough, opposite

Roll out the dough 3-mm (⅛-in) thick and fit into a buttered 23-cm (9-in) quiche, tart, or pie tin. Refrigerate while you prepare the filling.

Melt in a medium frying pan over medium heat:

30g (1oz) unsalted butter

Add:

900g (2lb) leeks, trimmed to white and tender green parts only, split lengthwise, cleaned thoroughly, and cut into slices 6-mm (¼-in) thick

½ tsp salt

Ground black pepper to taste

Cover and cook until the leeks are very soft, with little colour, stirring occasionally and reducing the heat as they cook, about 30 minutes. After about 15 minutes of cooking time, set a rack in the lowest position in the oven. Preheat the oven to 200°C (400°F) Gas 6.

For the custard, beat together until well combined:

2 large eggs

125ml (4floz) double or single cream

¼ tsp freshly grated or ground nutmeg

Salt and ground black pepper to taste

Remove the prepared pastry case from the refrigerator. When the leeks are done, add to the custard and transfer to the pastry case. Bake until golden and the custard is set, 20 to 30 minutes. Rest for 10 minutes to settle, then cut into wedges and serve.

LEEKS

Leeks are a member of the onion family. Leeks are in season from autumn to spring, but they are in the supermarket most of the year. When buying a bunch, try to choose leeks all the same size, preferably small. Be sure the leaves are bright, crisp, and not torn and the white parts are not discoloured. The layers of a leek can contain dirt, since the white stalks are "blanched", buried in earth to keep them pale. Rinse sliced leeks in a large bowl of cool water. Let them stand a few minutes while the dirt falls to the bottom, then lift them out with a strainer. Repeat if there is a lot of dirt left in the bowl. Store in perforated plastic vegetable bags in the refrigerator salad drawer.

Basic Breakfast Strata

6 to 8 servings

Sausage, cheese, vegetables, or whatever strikes your fancy gives this bread-based strata character and flavour. It can be left in the refrigerator overnight to settle, and baked the next morning while the coffee brews.

Butter a 2.5-litre (4-pint) soufflé dish or casserole. Heat a large, heavy frying pan over medium-high heat and add:

675g (1½ lb) bulk Country or Breakfast Sausage, 38, or shop-bought sausage

Brown the sausage for 5 minutes, breaking it up with a fork as it cooks. Add:

150g (5oz) sliced mushrooms

65g (2½ oz) finely chopped onions

Cook for 5 minutes, stirring often. Set aside. In a large bowl, combine:

4 large eggs, lightly beaten

500ml (16floz) milk

Have ready:

1 large loaf day-old Italian bread, cut into 18 to 20 slices, crusts removed, buttered if desired

Layer one-third of the bread in the bottom of the prepared baking dish. Top with half of the sausage mixture and sprinkle with one-third of:

120g (4oz) grated Swiss or Cheddar cheese

Repeat with another layer of bread, the other half of the sausage, and another 40g (1½ oz) cheese. Cover with a third layer of bread. Slowly pour the milk-and-egg mixture over the top and sprinkle with the last 40g (1½ oz) grated cheese. Let the strata stand for at least 1 hour or cover and refrigerate for up to 24 hours.

Preheat the oven to 180°C (350°F) Gas 4.

Set a baking sheet on the lowest rack of the oven to catch any drips and bake the strata until the top is nicely browned and bubbly, about 1 hour.

ABOUT
SIDE
DISHES

W*e love this grab-bag chapter for the ease and speed with which most of its dishes, elegant or plebeian, may be prepared.*

Many of the recipes on the following pages feature meat or seafood. Some of these, like Corned Beef Hash, 41, *or* Crabcakes, 42, *can star on their own at a special-occasion brunch or breakfast. Others provide classic robust accompaniments to breakfast egg dishes.*

Even more of the recipes in this chapter are strictly side dishes commonly served along with eggs. But what a marvelous variety they bring to the morning table! From classic Hash Brown Potatoes, 45, *to* Fried Green Tomatoes, 47, *and* Mushroom Ragout, 48, *they provide hosts and hostesses with a wealth of creativity for entertaining.*

Clockwise from left: *Sautéed Gammon Steak, 39; Hash Brown Potatoes, 45; Orange-Hazelnut Asparagus, 47*

Country or Breakfast Sausage

900g (2lb)

Fresh, raw sausages are best slowly pan-fried, or poached or simmered and then grilled or barbecued.

Cut into strips if using a meat grinder or 2.5-cm (1-in) dice if using a food processor:

675g (1½ lb) pork leg
225g (8 oz) pork back fat, trimmed of rind

Grind the meat and fat together in the meat grinder fitted with a 6-mm (¼-in) plate, or coarsely chop in the food processor. Mix together in a large bowl with:

2 tsp salt
2 tsp coarsely ground black pepper
1½ tsp dried sage
½ tsp dried marjoram
¼ tsp dried savory, crumbled
⅛ tsp ground ginger
Pinch of ground cloves
Pinch of ground cayenne
60ml (2 floz) cold water

Using your hands, knead and squeeze the mixture until well blended. Leave in bulk or form into cakes as needed. If not used immediately, fresh sausage can be frozen for up to 2 months.

MAKING SAUSAGE AT HOME

It is quite easy to make fresh, country-style (without casings) home-made sausage patties, especially with a food processor. The advantage of making your own sausage is that you control everything: the freshness, the amount of fat and salt, the quality and type of meat, the spice blend – the ultimate flavour.

When making sausage at home, remember these rules for safety and hygiene:

● Do not taste the raw meat mixture; instead, fry a small patty and taste that to check the seasonings.
● Keep the meat refrigerated before and between all steps.
● Do not leave any meat sitting in the grinder. Wash all utensils and equipment at once, even if you are only going to take a short break.
● Wash your hands frequently.
● If fresh sausage will not be eaten within 3 days, freeze it.

Chicken and Apple Sausage

About 900g (2lb)

This sausage can be used as a substitute for Country or Breakfast Sausage, above. Although it has less than half the fat of conventional breakfast sausage, it remains juicy if it is not overcooked. One of our favourite ways to serve these sausages is with French Toast, 58, smothered with Buttered Apple Slices, 56.

In a small saucepan, boil down to 2 to 3 tablespoons syrup:

250ml (8 floz) apple juice

Remove the bones from:

1kg (2¼ lb) chicken thighs

Cut the chicken into strips if using a meat grinder or 2.5-cm (1-in) dice if using a food processor. Grind the chicken and skin together in a meat grinder fitted with a 9-mm (⅜-in) plate, or coarsely chop by hand or in a food processor along with:

45g (1½ oz) dried apples

Mix the chicken and apple mixture and syrup in a large bowl with:

2½ tsp salt
1 tsp ground black pepper
1 tsp dried sage
½ tsp dried thyme
⅛ tsp ground cinnamon
⅛ tsp ground ginger

Using your hands, knead and squeeze the mixture until well blended. Leave in bulk or form into cakes as needed. If not used immediately, fresh sausage can be frozen for up to 2 months.

Sautéed Gammon Steak

4 servings

Melt in a large frying pan over medium-high heat:

10g (⅓ oz) unsalted butter

Add:

1 fully cooked gammon steak, 2- to 2.5-cm (¾- to 1-in) thick (675 to 900g/1½ to 2 lb)

Sauté the steak for 3 to 5 minutes each side. Remove and season with:

Ground black pepper to taste

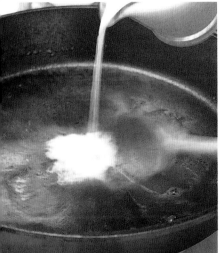

GAMMON STEAK WITH RED-EYE GRAVY

Prepare *Sautéed Gammon Steak, left*, cutting the slices 6- to 12-mm (¼- to ½-in) thick. After the gammon is cooked, remove it to a warmed platter and return the frying pan to the heat. Add 250ml (8floz) brewed coffee and boil, stirring, until it turns slightly red. Add 125ml (4floz) of whipping or double cream, reduce the heat, and simmer until slightly thickened, about 10 minutes. Season to taste.

HAM, BACON, AND CANADIAN BACON

The term ham is used for a variety of pork cuts from either the back leg or front shoulder that are processed through salt-curing and sometimes smoking and ageing.

Ham is usually labelled one of two ways: "Raw" or "Fully Cooked". Whichever you buy, follow scrupulously the packer's instructions on the label. Raw hams – also labelled "Cook Before Eating" – need to be roasted to an internal temperature of 68° to 70°C (155° to 160°F). Fully cooked hams – also called "Ready to Eat" or "Ready to Serve" – can be eaten as is.

Both raw and fully cooked hams come in several sizes and shapes. The whole ham, a 4.5- to 6.75-kg (10- to 15-lb) hind leg of pork with bone intact, is the most flavoursome and least wasteful cut. For smaller meals, you can buy a section of the whole ham, either the rounded part or lower leg half. The rounded half is somewhat more meaty but difficult to carve. Smaller steaks and ham roasts cut from the centre of the leg are also available.

Streaky bacon is made from trimmed pork bellies, also called sides, that have been cured in brine and then smoked until partially cooked. This is a fatty cut, and although there are leaner varieties (see below), the fat that remains is integral to its flavour and texture. Most bacon sold in supermarkets is sliced – thick or thin. Bacon loses flavour with time and should be used within a week or so of purchase. It can be frozen, but only for one or two months. When cooking bacon under the grill or in a frying pan, start with a cold grill or pan to prevent curling. Do not cook bacon over high heat, since it can go from browned to burnt in a matter of seconds. Separating slices of bacon in the pan as it warms helps prevent tearing of individual slices.

Canadian bacon – boneless pork loin that has been brine-cured and smoked – is obtainable from specialist butchers. Most Canadian bacon is pre-cooked, but it is also sold uncooked. Slice the cooked variety as you would regular ham. If Canadian bacon is not available, substitute back bacon.

Basic Pan-Grilled Steak

4 servings

Pan-grilling, or dry-sautéing, is a simple and convenient method for cooking any steak up to 5cm (2in) thick. It is especially useful for steaks less than 2cm (¾ in) thick, which fare poorly if grilled or barbecued. As an added advantage, pan-grilling is an excellent method for achieving a good crisp crust. It is important to get the pan hot enough that the meat sizzles the instant it hits the pan; lower temperatures will not produce the desired crust. The only disadvantage is that the high heat used for pan-grilling creates smoke and splattering, but this problem can be easily solved by opening a window or turning on the kitchen exhaust fan.

Pat dry:

4 small beef steaks (175 to 360g/ 6 to 12oz each) or 2 larger steaks (350 to 675g/¾ to 1½ lb each), 2 to 4cm (¾ to 1½ in) thick

If the meat is very lean, brush it with:

Olive oil

Season both sides of the steaks with:

Salt and ground black pepper to taste

Heat a large, heavy frying pan or griddle over medium-high heat. You may need 2 pans if the steaks are large. To determine when the pan is hot enough, touch a corner of the steak to the pan; it should sizzle briskly. Once the pan is hot, sear the steaks on one side, without crowding, for about 5 minutes. Turn them over and sear the other side for 3 to 4 minutes for rare, 5 to 8 minutes for medium. You may need to turn the steak more than once if one side gets too brown before the steak is done. Pour off any fat that accumulates during cooking.

PAN-GRILLING STEAK

Pan-grilling is best done in a well-seasoned heavy frying pan or griddle or non-stick frying pan. Specially designed ridged cast-iron pans are ideal but not necessary. Steaks should be patted dry and seasoned well with salt and pepper immediately before cooking: salting too far in advance makes the surface too moist for the meat to brown evenly. Season generously: pan-grilling is the technique used to produce spicy "blackened" steaks. With a well-seasoned pan, additional oil or fat is unnecessary when cooking well-marbled steaks. For leaner cuts, we recommend a light coating of vegetable oil. Do not overcrowd the pan. Cook steaks uncovered, turning them occasionally. Pour off any fat that accumulates to keep from frying the steaks.

Sautéed Bacon

When cooking bacon, cook to personal taste; the longer bacon cooks, the more fat is rendered out of it. Count on about 2 or 3 slices bacon per person.

Place in a large cast-iron or other heavy frying pan:

2 or 3 slices bacon per person

Do not overlap the slices; cook in batches if necessary. Place the pan over medium-low heat and slowly cook the bacon until browned. Turn the bacon often and monitor the heat to avoid burning the bacon. Spoon off the fat if over 6mm (¼ in) accumulates in the pan during cooking. Remove the slices to paper towels to drain.

Sautéed Canadian Bacon

Canadian bacon is boneless pork loin that has been brine-cured and smoked.

Melt in a large frying pan over medium heat:

10g (⅓oz) butter or 1½ tsp vegetable oil

Add:

2 or 3 slices Canadian bacon per person, 3 to 6mm (⅛ to ¼ in) thick

Cook the slices, turning often, until browned and heated through, 3 to 5 minutes. Remove to plates. Serve.

Corned Beef Hash

4 to 6 servings

The name of this beef is a reference to the corn-sized crystals of salt used to brine large cuts of beef brisket, sometimes with added allspice, black pepper, and bay leaves. The corned beef sold today is still a salt-and-spice brine-cured cut of beef brisket or round. In New England, it is still possible to find a "grey-cured" brisket, referring to the colour of corned beef made without chemicals to preserve its rosy colour. Corned beef is sold in vacuum-sealed bags that contain some of the brine and seasonings used during curing. It needs to be cooked before serving. New Englanders say that this hash must be put together from the leftovers of New England boiled dinner. It can also be made quite successfully with corned beef bought from a supermarket. Ask

for a slice that is thick enough to be cut into 1.2-cm (½-in) cubes. A well-seasoned cast-iron frying pan gives the hash a good brown crust, but a non-stick frying pan makes unmoulding easy. The quantities and pan size depend on the amount of leftovers you have, but here are approximate measurements.

Add to a large, heavy frying pan over medium-high heat:

3 tbsp vegetable oil

120g (4oz) chopped onions

Cook, stirring, until the onions are lightly browned, about 3 minutes. Add:

900g (2lb) cooked corned beef, cut into 1.2-cm (½-in) cubes

450g (1lb) cooked potatoes, cut into 1.2cm (½-in) cubes

RED FLANNEL HASH

Beetroot gives this hash its colour and its name.

Prepare *Corned Beef Hash*, left, adding 2 or 3 beetroot, cooked, peeled, and cut into 1.2-cm (½-in) cubes, to the other vegetables.

Stir once, reduce the heat to medium, and press down with a spatula to compress the hash. Cook, without disturbing, until the bottom is well browned, 10 to 15 minutes. Slide or invert the hash onto a serving plate. Garnish with:

Chopped fresh parsley

Serve with:

***Poached Eggs, 26,* or fried eggs**

Crabcakes

4 servings

Buy fresh lump crabmeat and give yourself time to refrigerate the cakes after you shape them so that they will hold together better when you cook them.
Gently pick over for bits of shell and cartilage:

450g (1lb) fresh lump crabmeat
In a frying pan over medium heat, warm:

30g (1oz) butter or 2 tbsp olive oil
When the butter foam has subsided, add:

1 tbsp finely diced red pepper (optional)
60g (2oz) diced spring onions
1 tsp finely chopped garlic
Cook, stirring, until the mixture is tender but not browned, about 10 minutes. Set aside. In a large bowl, mix the crabmeat with:

1 egg, lightly beaten
60ml (2 fl oz) mayonnaise
1 tbsp Dijon mustard

Salt and ground black pepper to taste
¼ tsp cayenne (optional)
4 tbsp finely chopped fresh parsley, coriander, or dill
2 tbsp fresh breadcrumbs, toasted
Add the sautéed vegetables and blend well. Place on a plate:

50 to 100g (2 to 3½ oz) fresh breadcrumbs, toasted
Shape the crab mixture into 8 small or 4 large cakes and, 1 at a time, coat each of the cakes in the breadcrumbs, pressing lightly to make sure they are coated evenly with crumbs. Place the cakes on a rack, or on a plate covered with greaseproof paper, and refrigerate for 1 to 2 hours if you have the time. When you are ready to cook, heat in a large frying pan over medium heat:

60g (2oz) butter or 4 tbsp *Clarified Butter*, 27, or oil
When the fat is hot, add the cakes, 1 at a time; do not crowd – it is fine to cook them in two batches. Adjust the heat so that the fat is sizzling but not burning the breadcrumbs. Rotate the cakes from side to side once or twice so that they brown evenly before turning them over after about 5 minutes. Cook until both sides are nicely browned; smaller cakes need a total of 8 to 10 minutes of cooking, larger ones 12 to15 minutes. Keep any finished cakes warm in a 150°C (300°F) Gas 2 oven while you complete the cooking. Serve hot with:

Lemon wedges or *Salsa Verde Cruda*, 49 (opposite)

Salmon Croquettes

4 servings

Combine in a medium bowl:
450g (1lb) cooked or tinned salmon
315g (11oz) mashed potatoes
60ml (2 fl oz) whipping or double cream
1 tbsp chopped fresh parsley
1 tsp snipped fresh chives
1 tsp snipped fresh dill
¼ tsp cayenne
Salt to taste
Spread in separate shallow bowls:
120g (4oz) fresh breadcrumbs
280g (10oz) plain flour
Whisk in a third shallow bowl:

4 large eggs
Shape the salmon mixture into 8 cakes. Working with 1 cake at a time, coat lightly with the flour and shake off the excess. Dip quickly into the eggs and let the excess drip off, then coat with the breadcrumbs. Heat in a large non-stick frying pan over medium heat until sizzling:

30g (1oz) unsalted butter
Add as many of the croquettes as will fit comfortably. Cook until golden on both sides, about 2 minutes each side. Remove and repeat with the remaining croquettes.

BUYING FISH

Buy fish from a fishmonger where you can see and smell the fish easily. Never buy fish that is not stored at 1°C (33°F). It should be on ice or in a refrigerated case with a thermometer. Good fish has firm, unmarred flesh and smells like fresh seawater. The surface of the fish should be bright, clear, and almost translucent. It should not have spots of pink (bruises) or brown (spoilage), and it should have no areas of deep red or brown.

Pommes Anna

6 to 8 servings

Position a rack in the centre of the oven. Preheat the oven to 220°C (425°F) Gas 7.
Have ready:
175g (6oz) butter, clarified, 27
Pour the butter into a Pommes Anna pan (opposite) or a 20-cm (8-in) cast-iron frying pan to a depth of 6mm (¼ in). Set over low heat and layer in:
1.2 to 1.35kg (2½ to 3lb) potatoes, peeled and in 3-mm (⅛-in) slices

Build the bottom layer especially carefully with overlapping, nicely shaped slices. As you assemble the slices, sprinkle each layer with:
Salt and ground black pepper to taste
Melted butter (optional)
When all the potatoes are in the pan, lightly butter or oil a saucepan lid slightly smaller than the pan, and press it firmly on top of the potatoes to compress them. Cover the pan

and put in the oven over a baking sheet to catch any drips. Bake for 20 minutes, remove the cover, and press down firmly on the potatoes. Bake, uncovered, until the sides are visibly browned and crisp, 20 to 25 minutes more. Holding the lid firmly against the potatoes, tilt the pan and pour off any melted butter that has not been absorbed. To serve, invert the potatoes onto a plate and cut into wedges.

Hash Brown Potatoes

4 servings

There are two kinds of hash browns: those made with raw potatoes and those made with boiled ones. The latter stick together better and cook more quickly, but some prefer the texture of those that begin raw.
Toss together:
675g (1½ lb) boiled or raw potatoes, peeled and finely diced
2 tbsp finely chopped onions (optional)
½ tsp salt

Ground black pepper to taste
Heat in a large, heavy frying pan over medium-high heat:
3 tbsp vegetable oil
Add the potatoes, toss them a few times, then spread them evenly in the pan and press down with a spatula. Reduce the heat to medium and cook slowly, pressing down several more times, until browned on the bottom, about 15 minutes. As the potatoes cook, give the pan a gentle

shake a few times to make sure they are not sticking. Cut the cake down the middle, then, using 2 spatulas, turn each side over. Do not worry if they do not turn evenly. If the pan seems too dry, add a little more oil before you return the potatoes. Cook the second side until golden brown. Serve piping hot.

Golden Potato Pancakes (Rösti)

2 or 3 servings

Rösti, the classic Swiss potato pancake, can be made with either raw or boiled potatoes.
Toss together:
450g (1lb) potatoes, cooked, peeled, and coarsely grated, or 450g (1lb) raw potatoes, peeled, cut into thin strips, rinsed, and dried
½ tsp salt

Melt in a medium, heavy frying pan over medium heat:
30g (1oz) butter
Add the potatoes and cook for 4 to 5 minutes, turning frequently so that the shreds are all lightly coated with butter. Press together to form a cake, reduce the heat to low, and cook until golden on the bottom, about 20 minutes. Turn the cake out

onto a plate, then slide it back into the pan and cook the second side. If desired, sprinkle the top with:
1½ tbsp grated Gruyère cheese
When the second side is golden, slide the potato cake onto a serving plate. Cut into 2 or 3 pieces and serve plain or garnished with:
Snipped fresh chives

Caramelized Onions

About 6 servings

If you cook onions over low heat so that they wilt without browning, they are said to be sweated. At this stage, their taste is gentle but not sweet. If you continue cooking, the onions will caramelize, or turn brown and quite sweet. The onions cook down to about half their volume and can be refrigerated for a few days or frozen.

Heat in a very large frying pan until the butter is melted:

30g (1oz) butter
2 tbsp olive oil

Add:

1.35kg (3lb) onions, thinly sliced
Sprinkle with:

1 tsp salt
Cook over the lowest possible heat for 1 hour, turning the onions several times. Do not be tempted to increase the heat – the onions need to be thoroughly soft before they begin to brown. Once they are soft, increase the heat to medium and cook, stirring constantly, until well browned, or caramelized, about 25 minutes

more. If the residue from the juices has built up in the pan, add:

125ml (4floz) dry white wine or water
Scrape the pan to dissolve the browned bits. They will immediately mix into the onions, darkening them further. Remove from the heat and season well with:

Salt and plenty of ground black pepper to taste
If serving as a side dish, you can add:

Grated Parmesan cheese (optional)

Fried Green Tomatoes

6 servings

Remove the stem ends, then cut crosswise into slices 1-cm (½-in) thick :

6 large green tomatoes

Combine in a shallow bowl:

320g (12oz) fine cornmeal
70g (2½ oz) plain flour
1 tbsp chopped fresh parsley
1 tbsp chopped fresh thyme
1 tsp paprika
Salt and ground black pepper
 to taste

Dip the tomato slices 1 at a time into:

250ml (8floz) milk

Then coat with the cornmeal mixture. Shake off the excess and set on a plate. Heat in a large frying pan until hot enough to sizzle a drop of water:

250ml (8floz) vegetable oil

Add the tomatoes in a single layer. Fry until golden and crisp, turning once. Repeat with the remaining tomatoes, adding oil as needed.

Kale with Bacon

2 to 4 servings

Strip the leaves from the stems, discard the stems, wash well, and coarsely chop:

1 large bunch kale (about
 450g/1lb)

Cook in a large frying pan until crisp, then remove to paper towels to drain:

1 or 2 slices bacon, diced

Pour off all but 1 tablespoon of the drippings, then add to the pan:

1 tbsp olive oil
1 small onion, finely chopped
1 clove garlic, chopped

Cook over medium heat until the onions are golden brown, then add as much kale as will fit in the pan and sprinkle with:

Salt

When the kale cooks down, add the rest. Cover and cook over medium heat until the kale is tender, 15 to 20 minutes. Season with:

Salt and ground black pepper
 to taste

Toss with the reserved bacon along with:

1 tbsp red wine vinegar

Orange-Hazelnut Asparagus

4 servings

Steam or boil:

450g (1lb) asparagus, bottoms
 snapped off

Place a large frying pan over medium heat and add:

30g (1oz) butter
1½ tbsp grated orange zest
Juice of ½ orange

25g (¾ oz) chopped hazelnuts,
 toasted

Cook until the butter is slightly browned, then add the cooked asparagus. Toss several times to heat through, then add:

Salt and ground black pepper
 to taste

Mushroom Ragout

4 servings

For more intense flavour, soak 15g (½ oz) dried mushrooms, chop, and add with the fresh mushrooms; use the soaking water for part of the liquid.
Heat over medium-high heat in a large saucepan:

1 tbsp olive oil

Add and cook until golden, about 10 minutes:

1 onion, diced

Remove and set aside. Heat in the same pan over medium heat:

1 tbsp olive oil

Add and cook until they begin to release their liquid:

450g (1lb) assorted fresh mush-rooms, wiped clean and thickly sliced

Add the onions along with:

2 cloves garlic, finely chopped

1 tsp chopped fresh rosemary, or scant ½ tsp dried

Salt and cracked black peppercorns to taste

Cook until the mushrooms begin to brown, another 3 to 4 minutes. Stir in:

1 tbsp tomato purée

Increase the heat to high and cook, stirring, for 1 to 2 minutes more. Add:

375ml (12floz) vegetable stock, chicken stock, or water

Reduce the heat and simmer for 10 minutes. Stir in to form a sauce:

30g (1oz) cold butter, cut into pieces

1½ tsp balsamic vinegar

Garnish with:

Grated Parmesan cheese (optional)

Chopped fresh parsley

Becker Duxelles

About 250ml (9floz)

Try this mushroom flavouring on toast, in scrambled eggs, or in omelettes.
Finely chop or process until they resemble coarse sand:

225g (8oz) mushrooms, wiped clean

Squeeze hard a small handful of the mushrooms at a time in dampened muslin or a thin cotton tea towel to extract their bitter juices. The mush-rooms will be in a solid lump if you have squeezed hard enough. Heat in a medium frying pan until the foam subsides:

30g (1oz) butter

3 tbsp olive oil

Add and cook briefly over medium heat until translucent:

60g (2oz) very finely chopped onions

2 cloves garlic, finely chopped

Add the mushrooms and cook, stir-ring often, over medium-high heat until they have begun to brown and there is very little liquid, 5 to 6 minutes. Stir in:

2 tbsp port or dry red wine

½ tsp ground black pepper

¼ tsp grated lemon zest

Cook until completely evaporated. Add:

60ml (2floz) whipping or double cream (optional)

Salt to taste

Pinch of dried thyme or grated or ground nutmeg

Let cool, then refrigerate in a cov-ered container for up to 10 days or freeze for up to 3 months.

MUSHROOMS

Mushrooms lend both elegance and earthiness to a dish. While we are grateful for the abundance of cultivated small button mush-rooms, wild mushrooms have con-siderably more character, and an assortment of them is available in greengrocers and supermarkets. Choose mushrooms that are heavy for their size, with dry, firm caps and stems – nothing damp or shrivelled, no dark or soft spots, and all close to the same size. If the gills are open, the mushrooms are more mature and their flavour will be stronger, and with a wild mushroom, this may be a plus. Open-gilled mushrooms should be used as soon as possible.

Wrap unwashed mushrooms in a loosely closed paper bag or wrap loosely in damp paper towels. Leave packaged mushrooms in their unopened package. Store on a refrigerator shelf, not in the salad drawer.

Clean mushrooms with a soft brush or wipe with a damp cloth. Or if the mushrooms are truly grimy, rinse them quickly under cold running water and pat dry.

Ratatouille

4 to 6 servings

This Provençal vegetable mélange can be served chilled with a splash of lemon juice or herb vinegar.

Sauté in a large frying pan or casserole over high heat until the vegetables are golden and just tender, 10 to 12 minutes:

60ml (2floz) olive oil

1 medium aubergine (about 450g/1lb), peeled and cut into 2.5cm (1-in) cubes

450g (1lb) courgette, cut into 2.5-cm (1-in) cubes

Remove the vegetables and reduce the heat to medium-high. In the same pan, cook until the onions are slightly softened:

2 tbsp olive oil

195g (7oz) sliced onions

Add and cook, stirring occasionally, until the vegetables are just tender but not browned, 8 to 12 minutes:

2 large red peppers, cut into 2.5-cm (1-in) squares

3 cloves garlic, chopped

Season with:

Salt and ground black pepper to taste

Add:

285g (10oz) chopped seeded peeled fresh tomatoes

2 or 3 sprigs fresh thyme

1 bay leaf

Reduce the heat to low, cover, and cook for 5 minutes. Add the aubergine and courgette and cook until everything is tender, about 20 minutes more. Taste and adjust the seasonings. Stir in:

4 tbsp chopped fresh basil

Sweetcorn Pudding Cockaigne

4 servings

For variation, add a little chopped fresh tarragon, thyme, basil, or mint.

Preheat the oven to 160°C (325°F) Gas 3. Butter a 20- x 20-cm (8- x 8-in) baking dish.

Cut and scrape the kernels from:

4 ears sweetcorn

Combine with:

1 tsp sugar (optional)

125 to 175ml (4 to 6floz) whipping or double cream

Salt and ground white pepper to taste

Spread the sweetcorn mixture in the baking dish. Dot the top with:

15g (½ oz) butter, cut into pieces

Bake until the pudding is set, 30 to 40 minutes.

PREPARING SWEETCORN

To remove kernels from the cob, hold the ear firmly with the bottom end placed in a shallow soup bowl to keep the kernels from splattering. Cut straight down the cob with a sharp knife, cutting two or three rows at a time.

Salsa Verde Cruda

About 500ml (16floz)

Intensely fresh, pungent, and herbal, this salsa is the easiest of all. It is especially good with eggs. Tomatillos, picked underripe, have a lemony tang that lends sprightliness to sauces in Mexican cooking. Since the onion is not rinsed and everything is whirled to a purée, the salsa must be served within an hour of preparing for optimum quality. If left to sit, the raw onion will overpower the sauce.

Combine in a food processor or blender and coarsely purée, leaving the mixture a little chunky:

225g (8oz) tomatillos, husked, rinsed, and coarsely chopped

1 small white or red onion, coarsely chopped

3 to 5 fresh green chilli peppers (such as serrano or jalapeño), seeded and coarsely chopped

1 clove garlic, peeled (optional)

3 to 4 tbsp fresh coriander sprigs

Remove to a medium bowl and stir in enough cold water to loosen the mixture to a sauce-like consistency. Stir in:

1 tsp salt, or to taste

¾ tsp sugar (optional)

Serve immediately.

ABOUT **PANCAKES,** WAFFLES, FRENCH TOAST & DOUGHNUTS

*P*erhaps no foods lend themselves to more occasions than those in this chapter. Not only can they all be served as breakfast or brunch main courses, but many may also be served as hors d'oeuvres, as luncheon or supper treats, or as desserts.

Many people like to cook pancakes, waffles, or French toast at the table, using auxiliary heat so that they reach guests in peak condition. Waffle irons, electric frying pans, or a double crêpe pan set, on which crêpes can be both cooked and sauced, are all tableside conveniences. In the kitchen, both cast-iron and non-stick griddles have their adherents.

No matter what your source of heat, be it a hot rock, an electric frying pan, or an automatic deep fryer for doughnuts, and no matter how fancy the name of the recipe you're preparing, all these confections are easily mixed and made from simple batters. There are three equally important things to control in producing them: the consistency of your batter, the surface of your griddle or pan, and the evenness of its heat. Follow the instructions on the following pages carefully to get the best results.

Dutch Baby, 56

Making Pancakes

Basic pancake batter is extremely simple – it contains nothing more than flour, leavening, and sugar (the dry ingredients) and milk, eggs, and melted butter (the wet ingredients) – and easy to mix.

To start, mix the dry ingredients in a bowl, stirring them together with a whisk to ensure that everything is well blended. There is rarely a need to sift dry ingredients, although you should always make sure that bicarbonate of soda and baking powder are free of lumps – if you find lumps, pinch them between your fingers. You can mix the dry ingredients in advance and store in a sealable plastic bag or an airtight container for up to 2 weeks in a cool cupboard or 1 month in the freezer.

The wet ingredients are mixed together in another bowl. You can mix the wet ingredients together ahead of time and store, covered, in the refrigerator for up to 24 hours.

When you are ready to make the pancakes, combine the dry and wet ingredients by mixing them, preferably with a rubber spatula or a wooden spoon, using a light hand and mixing only until the ingredients are combined. It is better to have a few small lumps than to overwork the batter, activate the flour's gluten and end up with a tough cake.

HOW TO COOK AMERICAN-STYLE PANCAKES

To begin, lightly butter, oil, or spray your griddle, if needed, and heat over medium heat. If you are using an electric griddle, preheat it to 180°C (350°F).

1 Pancake batter should be spooned, ladled, or poured slowly and steadily from a height of 5 to 8cm (2 to 3in) onto the griddle. To get a nice round pancake, hold the spoon, ladle, or jug steady so that the batter falls in the same spot. Depending on the consistency of the batter, it will either spread into a round by itself or need a little nudge with the back of a ladle or spoon or a metal spatula. It is always a good idea to make one test pancake first to check the batter's consistency and judge how much space each one will need. If, for example, a recipe produces 10-cm (4-in) round pancakes, you will need to pour the batter onto the griddle at intervals of 12 to 15cm (5 to 6in). Of course, if a couple of pancakes run together, it is not a tragedy, since they can be cut apart easily with the edge of a spatula.

2 Most pancakes are "bubblers". When the top of the pancake is speckled with bubbles, some bubbles have popped, and the underside of the pancake is golden brown (lift an edge with your spatula and peek at the underside to make sure), slide your spatula under the pancake and turn it, taking care not to let it fold over on itself.

3 Cook the pancake until the second side is lightly browned (lift an edge with your spatula) – it won't get as dark as the first side – which will take only about half as long as the first side did. It is best to turn pancakes just once.

Basic American Pancakes

About twelve 12-cm (5-in) cakes

Prepare and preheat your griddle, opposite.

Whisk together in a large bowl:

210g (7½ oz) plain flour
3 tbsp sugar
1½ tsp baking powder
½ tsp salt

Whisk together in another bowl:

375ml (12floz) milk
45g (1½ oz) unsalted butter, melted
2 large eggs
½ tsp vanilla extract (optional)

Pour the wet ingredients over the dry ingredients and gently stir them together, mixing just until combined. If you wish, fold in one or more of the following:

80g (3oz) plump raisins or other very finely diced soft dried fruit
60g (2oz) fresh or frozen blueberries
60g (2oz) chopped nuts, toasted
100g (3½ oz) thinly sliced ripe banana
40g (1½ oz) crumbled cooked bacon
40g (1½ oz) grated cheese
20g (scant 1oz) shredded sweetened dried coconut
25g (1oz) grated plain or milk chocolate

Spoon 80ml (3floz) batter onto the griddle for each pancake, nudging the batter into rounds. Cook until the top of each pancake is speckled with bubbles and some bubbles have popped open, then turn and cook until the underside is lightly browned. Serve immediately or keep warm in a 95°C (200°F) Gas ¼ oven while you finish cooking the rest. Serve with:

Pure maple syrup or honey
Pats of butter

BUTTERMILK

Buttermilk, once the residue left over from making butter, is today made by adding a bacterial culture to skimmed milk to produce the flavour, body, and acidity of the original product. Thus the word "buttermilk" today means cultured buttermilk.

BASIC BUTTERMILK PANCAKES

Serve these pancakes at your next brunch with seasonal fruit and pure maple syrup.
Prepare *Basic Pancakes, left,* adding ½ teaspoon bicarbonate of soda to the dry ingredients and substituting buttermilk for the milk.

Cornmeal Pancakes

About sixteen 12-cm (5-in) cakes

Prepare and preheat your griddle, opposite.

Whisk together in a large bowl:

200g (7oz) yellow cornmeal, preferably stone ground
150g (5oz) plain flour
1¾ tsp baking powder
¾ tsp salt

Whisk together in another bowl:

410ml (13floz) milk
60g (2oz) unsalted butter, melted
60ml (2floz) pure maple syrup
2 large eggs

Pour the wet ingredients over the dry ingredients and gently whisk them together, mixing just until combined. The batter will be very thin. Stir in:

115g (4oz) fresh, frozen, or drained tinned sweetcorn kernels

Spoon 60ml (2½ floz) batter onto the griddle for each pancake, leaving room for spreading. This is a thin, runny batter that forms irregularly shaped rounds before it sets, but the pancakes will look fine when you flip them over. Cook until the top of each pancake is speckled with bubbles and some bubbles have popped, then turn and cook until the underside is lightly browned. Serve immediately or keep warm in a 95°C (200°F) Gas ¼ oven while you finish cooking the rest. Serve with:

Pure maple syrup or honey
Yogurt

JALAPEÑO CORNMEAL PANCAKES

Jalapeños are widely available and can vary considerably in their heat from totally mild to the quite hot varieties found in some supermarkets and their homeland of Veracruz, Mexico.
For a spicy, savoury pancake, prepare *Cornmeal Pancakes, left,* folding into the batter 1 fresh jalapeño pepper, seeded and finely chopped, 2 tablespoons finely chopped fresh coriander (optional), ½ teaspoon hot red pepper sauce, ¼ teaspoon chilli powder, and ground black pepper to taste.

Lemon Pancakes

About twelve 10-cm (4-in) cakes

These can also be served with honey.

Prepare and preheat your griddle, 52.
Whisk together in a large bowl:

140g (4½ oz) plain flour
60g (2oz) sugar
1½ tsp baking powder
½ tsp bicarbonate of soda
¼ tsp salt

Whisk together in another bowl:

175ml (6floz) sour cream
80ml (3floz) milk
60ml (2floz) fresh lemon juice

45g (1½ oz) unsalted butter,
** melted**
1 large egg
1½ tsp vanilla extract

Pour the wet ingredients over the dry ingredients and gently whisk them together, mixing just until combined. Fold in:

Finely grated zest of 2 lemons

The batter will be thick and bubbly – similar to a cake batter. Spoon 60ml (2floz) batter onto the griddle for each pancake, nudging the batter into rounds. Cook until the top of each pancake is speckled with bubbles and some bubbles have popped, then turn and cook until the underside is lightly browned. Serve immediately or keep warm in a 95°C (200°F) Gas ¼ oven while you finish cooking the rest. Serve with (opposite):

Sweetened sour cream or *Crème Fraîche*, 87

KEEPING PANCAKES HOT

Pancakes can be kept in a preheated 95°C (200°F) Gas ¼ oven for up to 20 minutes before serving. As they come off the griddle, place them on a heatproof platter, one slightly overlapping the last, and cover them very loosely with foil. For added tenderness and moistness, brush both sides of each pancake with melted butter before putting it in the oven.

LEMON POPPY SEED PANCAKES

Unless organic, citrus fruits are usually coated with wax. If using the zest, we urge you to use organic fruits. Avoid citrus with deep bruises, soft spots, or mould. In grating zest, remove only the top coloured layer, as the white pith beneath is bitter. Prepare Lemon Pancakes, above, folding in 70g (2½ oz) poppy seeds along with the lemon zest.

Blueberry Buttermilk Pancakes

About twelve 11.5-cm (4½-in) cakes

Prepare and preheat your griddle, 52.
Whisk together in a large bowl:

140g (4½ oz) plain flour
80g (3oz) yellow cornmeal,
** preferably stone ground**
45g (1½ oz) sugar
1¼ tsp baking powder
¼ tsp bicarbonate of soda
¼ tsp salt

Whisk together in another bowl:

310ml (10floz) buttermilk
60g (2oz) unsalted butter,
** melted**

2 large egg yolks
1½ tsp finely grated lemon zest

Pour the wet ingredients over the dry ingredients and gently whisk them together, mixing just until combined. Beat until the peaks are stiff but not dry, then fold into the batter:

2 large egg whites

Fold in:

120g (4oz) fresh or frozen
** blueberries**

Spoon 80ml (3floz) batter onto the griddle for each pancake, nudging the batter into rounds. Cook until the top of each pancake is speckled with bubbles and some bubbles have popped, then turn and cook until the underside is lightly browned. Serve immediately or keep warm in a 95°C (200°F) Gas ¼ oven while you finish cooking the rest. Serve with:

Pure maple syrup, honey, or
** blueberry sauce**

Silver Dollar Hots

About 40 mini pancakes

Super light and fluffy describes these delicate treats. Hot off the griddle is the best way to eat them. You can use a platar, a cast-iron pan with round indentations, for perfectly shaped cakes. Prepare and preheat your griddle, 52. Lightly beat:

2 large eggs
Whisk in:
250ml (8floz) sour cream
35g (1½ oz) plain flour
1½ tbsp sugar

½ tsp salt
¼ tsp bicarbonate of soda
Spoon 1 tablespoon batter onto the griddle for each pancake, nudging the batter into 6.5-cm (2½-in) rounds. Cook until the top of each pancake is speckled with bubbles and some bubbles have popped, then turn over and cook until the underside is lightly browned. Serve immediately with:
Pure maple syrup or fresh fruit

Dutch Baby

One 25-cm (10-in) cake; 2 to 4 servings

Serve this straight from the oven with a dusting of icing sugar, a spoonful of the best fruit preserves you can lay your hands on, or Buttered Apple Slices, below.
Preheat oven to 220°C (425°F) Gas 7. Whisk together until smooth:
125ml (4floz) milk
70g (2½ oz) plain flour
45g (1½ oz) sugar
2 large eggs, at room temperature
Melt in a 25-cm (10-in) ovenproof

frying pan (cast iron is ideal) over medium heat:
40g (1½ oz) unsalted butter
Tilt the pan so that the butter coats the sides. Pour the egg mixture into the pan and cook, without stirring, for 1 minute. Place the pan in the oven and bake until the pancake is puffed and golden, 12 to 15 minutes. Serve quickly, for the pancake loses its puff, and therefore its drama, almost immediately.

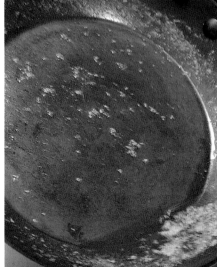

Buttered Apple Slices

4 breakfast servings; 8 garnish servings

Melt in a large frying pan over medium-low heat until foamy:
30g (1oz) butter
Add in a single layer:
2 firm, tart apples, cored and cut into 1-cm (⅜-in) slices
Cook until the bottoms are golden. Turn and cook the second side until

golden, a few minutes longer, depending on the firmness of the apples. Do not let them turn soft.
To glaze, especially if they are very tart, sprinkle over the surface:
2 tbsp sugar
Let stand until the sugar melts. Serve warm.

Raised Buckwheat Blini

About fifteen 8-cm (3-in) pancakes

Combine in a saucepan:

375ml (12floz) milk

60g (2oz) unsalted butter

Heat until the butter is melted, then let cool to between 40° and 46°C (105° and 115°F). Sprinkle with:

2 tsp active dry yeast

Let stand until the yeast is dissolved, about 5 minutes. Whisk together:

90g (3oz) plain flour

90g (3oz) buckwheat flour

2 tbsp sugar

1 tsp salt

Pour the wet ingredients over the dry ingredients and gently whisk them together, mixing just until combined. Cover the bowl tightly with cling film and let rise in a warm place until doubled in volume, about 1 hour. When the batter has risen, you can make the pancakes immediately or refrigerate the covered bowl for up to 24 hours. If the batter is refrigerated, let stand at room temperature for 20 minutes before proceeding.

Stir to deflate the batter and whisk in:

3 large eggs, lightly beaten

Prepare and preheat your griddle, 52. Spoon a scant 60ml (2floz) batter onto the griddle for each pancake, leaving room between the pancakes for spreading. Cook until the top of each blini is speckled with bubbles and some bubbles have popped, then turn and cook until the underside is lightly browned. Serve immediately or keep warm in a 95°C (200°F) Gas ¼ oven while you finish cooking the rest. Serve with:

Melted butter or smoked salmon and sour cream or *Crème Fraîche*, 87, or pure maple syrup

Making French Toast

The British and Americans eat French toast (or eggy bread) for breakfast, but the French serve it for dessert (and call it *pain perdu*, or "lost bread"). White bread makes the lightest French toast, but whole-wheat and rye breads work too. Not surprisingly, French bread is fine for this dish, and brioche and croissants are superb. Home cooks have developed a number of variations on the basic theme, such as stuffing French toast with a rich filling, baking it with a honey glaze, and even soaking the bread overnight, then baking it to golden goodness the following day.

French Toast

6 slices

When hungry breakfasters call out for French toast, this is what they hope they will get.

Whisk together in a shallow bowl:

160ml (5½ floz) whole milk or double or single cream

4 large eggs

2 tbsp sugar or pure maple syrup

1 tsp vanilla extract

¼ tsp salt

One or two at a time, add:

6 slices white or egg bread, with or without crusts

Turn the slices in the egg mixture until thoroughly saturated but not falling apart. In a frying pan, melt over medium heat:

30g (1oz) unsalted butter

Add as many slices of bread to the pan as will fit without crowding and cook until the underside is golden brown. Turn the bread and cook until the second side is golden. Serve immediately or keep warm in a 95°C (200°F) Gas ¼ oven while you finish cooking the rest. Dust each slice with:

Icing sugar

and serve with:

Pure maple syrup

Bacon, ham, or sausages

MAPLE SYRUP

Maple syrup is boiled-down sap from sugar maple trees. Only pure maple syrup can be labelled as such. Largely sucrose with some invert sugar, the best grades are light in colour. It is often stored covered at room temperature, but after it is opened it must be stored in the refrigerator to inhibit mould growth. Should the syrup crystal-lize, set the jar in hot water.

Honey-Bun French Toast

6 slices

Preheat the oven to 200°C (400°F) Gas 6.

In a 30- x 23-cm (12- x 9-in) glass baking dish, place:

60g (2oz) unsalted butter

3 tbsp honey

Heat in the oven until the butter is melted and the honey is bubbling. Do not allow the mixture to take on any colour. Remove the pan from the oven, stir to mix the honey and butter, and sprinkle over the surface:

100g (3½ oz) chopped pecans

While the butter and honey are melting, whisk together in a shallow bowl:

160ml (5½ floz) apple juice

4 large eggs

¼ tsp ground cinnamon

¼ tsp salt

Pinch of ground allspice (optional)

One or two at a time, add:

6 thick slices white or egg bread, with or without crusts

Turn the slices in the egg mixture until thoroughly saturated but not falling apart. Arrange the soaked bread over the nuts in the baking pan. Bake until the top is golden brown and the bottom is bubbly, 15 to 20 minutes. Serve immediately with:

Honey or pure maple syrup

Filled French Toast

8 slices

For variety, mix the cream cheese with thick fruit preserves or spiced apple butter.

Preheat the oven to 200°C (400°F) Gas 6. Lightly butter a baking sheet. Whisk together:

225g (8oz) cream cheese, softened
50g (2oz) light brown sugar
60ml (2floz) honey or pure maple syrup
1 tsp vanilla extract
Grated zest of ½ orange (optional)
Pinch of ground cinnamon
Pinch of salt

Stir in:

30g (1oz) finely chopped nuts (e.g. almonds or pecans), toasted, or shredded sweetened or unsweetened dried coconut (optional)

Trim the crusts from:

One 450-g (1-lb) loaf white bread, preferably egg bread

Cut the loaf into slices 2.5-cm (1-in) thick; you will probably get 8 slices. Carefully work the knife into one side of each slice of bread to create a pocket that you can open with your fingers. Spoon an equal amount of filling into each pocket. Whisk together in a shallow bowl:

250ml (8floz) milk
3 large eggs
35g (1½ oz) plain flour
3 tbsp sugar
2 tsp baking powder
2 tsp vanilla extract
¼ tsp salt

One or two slices at a time, soak the bread in the egg mixture until thoroughly saturated but not falling apart. In a frying pan, heat over medium-low:

15g (½ oz) unsalted butter
1 tbsp vegetable oil

Add as many slices of bread to the pan as will fit without crowding and cook until the underside is just lightly golden. Turn the bread and cook until the second side is lightly golden. As each slice is cooked, transfer it to the baking sheet. Continue cooking the French toast, adding more butter and oil as needed. Bake the sautéed slices until puffed and beautifully golden, about 6 minutes. Serve immediately with:

Icing sugar, maple syrup, or honey

Overnight Baked French Toast

8 slices

A great dish when guests are expected the next morning for brunch. The overnight soak produces very creamy and fluffy French toast.

Whisk together in a 20- x 20-cm (8- x 8-in) baking dish:

250ml (8floz) cream or whole milk
6 large eggs
60ml (2floz) pure maple syrup
2 tbsp light brown sugar
1 tsp vanilla extract
¼ tsp salt

Trim the crusts from:

8 slices white or egg bread

One slice at a time, turn the bread over in the egg mixture to coat it, then fit the coated bread into the dish in a double layer. Very gently press the bread with the back of a fork to compress the slices slightly. Cover with cling film and press on the plastic to help the bread soak up the egg mixture. Refrigerate overnight.

Preheat the oven to 200°C (400°F) Gas 6. Lightly butter a baking sheet, preferably non-stick.

Using a wide spatula, lift the bread, slice by slice, out of the soaking mixture, allowing the excess liquid to drip back into the dish, and place on the baking sheet. Bake until puffed and golden, 12 to 15 minutes, turning the slices over halfway through the baking. Serve immediately with:

Pure maple syrup
Sliced fresh fruit (optional)

EGGLESS MAPLE FRENCH TOAST

6 slices

Trim the crusts from 6 slices white or egg bread. Measure 175ml (6floz) pure maple syrup. Brush 1 tablespoon of the syrup over each side of each slice of bread, stacking the slices on top of each other on a plate. Cover with greaseproof paper and gently press on the paper to help the bread soak up the syrup. Let stand for about 5 minutes. In a frying pan, melt 30g (1oz) unsalted butter over medium heat until bubbly. Add the slices of syrup-soaked bread. Cook until golden and crispy on both sides, adding more butter as needed.

Making Waffles

Waffles are light, leavened cousins of the ancient Communion wafer, which, like waffles, were once baked in irons and had the same honeycomb pattern that characterizes all members of the wafer/waffle family. The earliest waffle irons were probably produced in thirteenth-century Germany or Holland. Consisting of two hinged iron plates attached to long wooden handles, the irons were designed to be held over the embers of a hearth fire. The ancient plates were far more elaborate than those of today's waffle irons, often embossed with family initials, religious symbols, coats of arms, figures, or landscape scenes.

Today, the usual pattern is simply a grid, often shallow but better, especially for Belgian waffles, when deep. Most contemporary waffle irons are square or rectangular in shape, but look for those shaped like a Five of Hearts – a circle composed of five shallow-gridded hearts – a form once popular among the Pennsylvania Dutch. Waffles were brought to America by the Dutch settlers of the 1600s, but they were probably not widely known until sometime in the next century. In the late 1700s, Thomas Jefferson travelled to France and brought back a French waffle iron at considerable trouble and expense.

A waffle batter needs butter and a fair amount of it. The butter both tenderizes a waffle and helps keep it from sticking to the iron. You can substitute oil for butter in a recipe without changing the texture – of course, this will affect the flavour – but you cannot make waffles without either butter or oil.

HOW TO BAKE WAFFLES

You can bake any waffle recipe in any waffle iron, but the amount of batter you will need for each waffle and the number of waffles the recipe yields will change. In all likelihood, in fact, you will have to make adjustments for your own iron – you may need less of a thinner batter, more of a thicker one.

1 Try a sample waffle or two to be safe. Because batters have different consistencies, some will spread across the iron's grids by themselves.

2 Others will need a little cajoling with the back of a metal spatula, wooden spoon, or ladle.

Batters should be poured or spread to within 6mm (¼ in) of the edge of the grids; when the iron is closed, the top plate will push the batter to the edge to fill the space. If you have overfilled the grids or spread the batter too far, try baking with the iron open for 30 seconds; this may stop any overflow. Once the iron is closed, do not open it until the steam has subsided. Waffles usually take 4 to 5 minutes to cook. If after that time the lid is difficult to open, do not force it, for the waffle is not yet baked.

USING A WAFFLE IRON

If you are using a stove-top cast-iron waffler, seasoning is a must. Rub the baking surfaces lightly with corn or peanut oil and wipe off any excess oil. If you have an electric waffle iron with a non-stick finish, there is probably no need to season the grids; simply follow the manufacturer's instructions. Even if seasoning is not required, the iron may smoke when it is first heated. This is normal. A properly seasoned waffle iron, with or without a non-stick coating, doesn't need to be greased every time you use it, since most waffle batters contain enough butter to keep the waffles from sticking. If you feel it is necessary to grease your iron, rub with corn or peanut oil, vegetable oil spray, or melted butter before heating the iron.

Basic Waffles

Twelve 15-cm (6-in) waffles

We give you three choices to prepare this recipe: use 60g (2oz) butter for a reduced-fat waffle; 115g (4oz) for a classic light and fluffy waffle; or 225g (8oz) for the crunchiest, most delicious waffle imaginable. To toast nuts in the oven: spread them blanched or unblanched on an ungreased baking sheet and bake in a 160°C (325°F) Gas 3 oven for 5 to 7 minutes. Check and stir often to prevent burning.

Preheat your waffle iron.

Whisk together in a large bowl:

245g (9oz) plain flour
1 tbsp baking powder
1 tbsp sugar
½ tsp salt

Whisk together in another bowl:

3 large eggs, well beaten
60 to 225g (2 to 8oz) unsalted butter, melted
375ml (12floz) milk

Make a well in the centre of the dry ingredients and pour in the wet ingredients. Gently whisk them together with a few swift strokes. (The batter should have a pebbled look, similar to a muffin batter.) If you wish, fold in one or more of the following:

80g (3oz) plump raisins or other very finely diced soft dried fruit
60g (2oz) fresh or frozen blueberries or raspberries
50g (2oz) finely chopped nuts, toasted
½ ripe banana, thinly sliced
35g (1½ oz) crumbled cooked bacon
35g (1½ oz) grated cheese
20g (¾ oz) shredded sweetened dried coconut
25g (1oz) grated plain or milk chocolate

Spoon 125ml (4floz) batter (or the amount recommended by your waffle iron's manufacturer) onto the hot iron. Spread the batter to within 6mm (¼ in) of the edge of the grids with the back of a metal spatula, wooden spoon, or ladle. Close the lid and bake until the waffle is golden brown (see *How to Bake Waffles, opposite*). Serve immediately or keep warm while you cook the rest. Serve with:

Pure maple syrup or jam
Pats of butter
or:
Hot Buttered Maple Sauce, below

BASIC BUTTERMILK WAFFLES

Prepare *Basic Waffles, above*, adding ¼ teaspoon bicarbonate of soda to the dry ingredients and substituting buttermilk for the milk.

Hot Buttered Maple Sauce

About 330ml (11floz); 6 to 8 servings

When drenched with this sauce, waffles become a showpiece.

Combine in a medium, heavy saucepan:

250ml (8floz) pure maple syrup
60g (2oz) sugar

Stirring constantly with a wooden spoon, bring to a boil and cook until the last drop of sauce that falls from the spoon spins a short, wispy thread. This will take about 3 minutes. Remove from the heat and add:

85g (3oz) unsalted butter, cut into pieces
2 tbsp water
⅛ tsp salt

Stir briskly until the butter is melted and the sauce is thick and creamy. Whisk in a bowl until light and frothy:

1 large egg

Slowly whisk the hot maple mixture into the egg. Rinse out the pan, dissolving any sugar crystals, then dry the pan thoroughly. Return the sauce to the pan and cook, stirring constantly, over medium heat until the sauce comes to a simmer and is thickened. Serve at once, or let cool then cover and refrigerate for up to 3 days. Reheat over low heat, stirring; if the sauce separates, remove from the heat and whisk in a little hot water.

KEEPING WAFFLES WARM

If you are preparing a large breakfast or brunch, you may want to bake waffles ahead of time. Waffles can be kept warm for as long as 20 minutes in a 95°C (200°F) Gas ¼ oven. Spread the waffles out in a single layer directly on the oven rack. It is important not to stack waffles, which makes them soggy. Because waffles freeze and reheat well, we plan for leftovers and multiply the recipe, wrapping cooled waffles airtight and storing them in the freezer. To reheat, place the still-frozen waffles directly on the rack of a preheated 180°C (350°F) Gas 4 oven and bake until heated through, about 10 minutes.

Belgian Waffles

Twelve 15-cm (6-in) waffles

When Belgian waffles were introduced to Americans at the 1964 World's Fair in New York City, they were yeast-raised and served with sweetened whipped cream. This recipe is in the spirit of the original Belgian waffle.

Whisk together:

2¼ tsp active dry yeast
60ml (2floz) warm (40° to 46°C/ 105° to 115°F) milk

Let stand until the yeast is dissolved, about 5 minutes. Whisk together in a large bowl:

3 large egg yolks
60ml (2floz) lukewarm milk
170g (6oz) unsalted butter, melted and cooled to lukewarm

Whisk in the yeast mixture along with:

100g (3½ oz) sugar
1½ tsp salt
2 tsp vanilla extract

Add, in 3 parts:

560g (1¼ lb) plain flour

alternating, in 2 parts, with:

625ml (1 pint) warm (40° to 46°C/105° to 115°F) milk

Beat until soft peaks form, then fold into the batter:

3 large egg whites

Cover the bowl tightly with cling film and let rise in a warm place until doubled in volume, about 1 hour. Stir to deflate the batter. Preheat your waffle iron. Spoon 125ml (4floz) batter (or the amount recommended by your waffle iron's manufacturer) onto the hot iron. Spread the batter to within 6mm (¼ in) of the edge of the grids, using the back of a metal spatula, wooden spoon, or ladle. Close the lid and bake until the waffle is golden brown (see *How to Bake Waffles*, 60). Serve immediately or keep warm in a single layer on a rack in a 95°C (200°F) Gas ¼ oven while you finish cooking the rest.

Serve with:

Pats of butter and icing sugar or fresh fruit and whipped cream

Cornmeal Waffles

Eight 16-cm (6½-in) round waffles

These can be thought of as flat, crisp corn bread.

Preheat your waffle iron.

Whisk together in a large bowl:

140g (5oz) plain flour

160g (5½ oz) cornmeal, preferably stone ground

2 tsp baking powder

¾ tsp salt

½ tsp bicarbonate of soda

Whisk together in another bowl:

500ml (16floz) buttermilk

60ml (2floz) pure maple syrup

75g (3oz) unsalted butter, melted

2 large egg yolks, at room temperature

Pour the wet ingredients over the dry ingredients and gently whisk them together, mixing just until com-

bined. Beat until the peaks are stiff but not dry, then fold into the batter:

2 large egg whites

Spoon 125ml (4floz) batter (or a little more than the amount recommended by your waffle iron's manufacturer) onto the hot iron. Spread the batter to within 6mm (¼ in) of the edge of the grids, using the back of a metal spatula, wooden spoon, or ladle. Close the lid and bake until the waffle is golden brown (see *How to Bake Waffles*, 60). Serve immediately or keep warm in a single layer on a rack in a 95°C (200°F) Gas ¼ oven while you finish cooking the rest. Serve with:

Pure maple syrup

Bacon

Honey Bran Waffles

Six 16-cm (6½-in) round waffles

Wholewheat flour and coarse bran, also known as miller's bran, are available at health food shops. Try these with slices of mature Cheddar cheese.

Preheat your waffle iron.

Whisk together in a large bowl:

110g (4oz) plain flour

110g (4oz) wholewheat flour

30g (1oz) coarse bran

2 tsp baking powder

½ tsp salt

¼ tsp bicarbonate of soda

Whisk together in another bowl:

375ml (12floz) buttermilk

80ml (3floz) honey

60g (2oz) unsalted butter, melted

2 large eggs

½ tsp vanilla extract

Pour the wet ingredients over the

dry ingredients and gently whisk them together, mixing just until combined. The batter will be thick and bubbly. Spoon 125ml (4floz) batter (or a little more than the amount recommended by your waffle iron's manufacturer) onto the hot iron. Spread the batter to within 6mm (¼ in) of the edge of the grids, using the back of a metal spatula, wooden spoon, or ladle. Close the lid and bake until the waffle is golden brown (see *How to Bake Waffles*, 60). Serve immediately or keep warm in a single layer on a rack in a 95°C (200°F) Gas ¼ oven while you finish cooking the rest. Serve with:

Honey or pure maple syrup

Pats of butter

Making Crêpes and Blintzes

Crêpes were taken to America by the English settlers of the seventeenth century and continued to be enjoyed until the time of the Civil War. Early Americans knew crêpes by their old English name, pancakes, which in the late 1800s became the usual name for the puffy, chemically leavened griddle cakes so beloved across America today. As fluffy pancakes soared in popularity in the late nineteenth century, crêpes became rare in the American scene until the 1930s, when they were reintroduced from France, primarily as the famous crêpes Suzette. Since then, their fortunes have risen, then fallen, then risen again. But in one form or another, they appear to be here to stay.

The batters for crêpes and blintzes are thinner than those used for pancakes and are best made at least 30 minutes ahead so that the flour can absorb all the liquid. Batters can be made up to 2 days ahead, in fact, and kept in a bowl, covered, in the refrigerator. Give the batter a good stirring before you start.

Crêpes and blintzes are most easily made in a crêpe pan – a short-sided frying pan about 19cm (7½ in) across. (You can also use a regular frying pan of the same size.) If your pan is non-stick, you may not have to season it – simply follow the manufacturer's instructions. New crêpe pans always need to be seasoned. Rub the cooking surface lightly with corn or peanut oil, then wipe off any excess. Once seasoned, crêpe pans do not have to be washed; a quick wipe with a paper towel should keep them in good shape.

HOW TO MAKE CRÊPES AND BLINTZES

You'll need only 2 to 3 tablespoons of batter for each crêpe or blintz.

1 Heat a crêpe pan over medium to medium-high heat and grease it lightly by rubbing a small piece of butter on the cooking surface.

2 Lift the pan off the heat and pour in 2 to 3 tablespoons of the batter, tilting and rotating the pan so that the batter covers the entire bottom in a very thin, even layer. It is an odd movement, but you will get the hang of it after a crêpe or two.

3 Cook the crêpe on one side until it sets and starts to bubble (the underside should be golden brown).

4 Run a blunt, thin knife or palette knife around the edge of the pan, lift the crêpe up, and turn it over. (If you can stand the heat, fingers are the best tools for turning.) Cook the second side just until it is speckled with golden dots; it will never be as brown as the first side. For blintzes, cook just the first side. Crêpes and blintzes can be served as soon as they are made or stored for later use.

Basic Sweet Crêpes

About twelve 19-cm (7½-in) crêpes

Combine in a blender or food processor until smooth:

75g (3oz) plain flour
125ml (4floz) milk
60ml (2floz) lukewarm water
2 large eggs
30g (1oz) unsalted butter, melted
1½ tbsp sugar
Pinch of salt

Pour the batter into a jug or other container with a pouring lip. Cover with cling film and let stand for 30 minutes or refrigerate for up to 2 days. (This allows the flour to thoroughly absorb the liquid and gives the gluten in the flour a chance to relax.)

Place a non-stick or seasoned crêpe pan over medium heat. Coat the pan with a little:

Unsalted butter

Stir the batter and pour about 2 tablespoons into the pan, lifting the pan off the heat and tilting and rotating it so that the batter forms an even, very thin layer. Cook until the top is set and the underside is golden. Turn the crêpe over, using a spatula or your fingers (fingers work best here) and cook until the second side is lightly browned. Remove the crêpe to a piece of greaseproof paper. Continue cooking the rest of the crêpes, buttering the pan and stirring the batter before starting each one. Stack the finished crêpes between sheets of greaseproof paper. Use immediately or allow to cool, wrap airtight, and freeze for up to 1 month.

Crêpes with Caramelized Apples

12 crêpes; 6 servings

For the apple syrup, stir together in a small saucepan:

250ml (8floz) fresh apple juice
3 tbsp light corn syrup or golden syrup
1 tbsp light brown sugar
1 tbsp fresh lemon juice

Bring to a boil, then reduce the heat to medium and boil, stirring occasionally, until the mixture is reduced by half, about 10 minutes. Remove from the heat and swirl in, piece by piece:

30g (1oz) cold unsalted butter, cut into 6 pieces

Serve immediately or let cool, pour into a jar, and refrigerate for up to 1 week. Reheat (but do not boil) before using.

Peel, halve, and core:

3 Golden Delicious or other firm, sweet apples (450 to 550g/ 1 to 1¼ lb)

Cut each half into 6 wedges. In a large frying pan, preferably non-stick, melt over medium heat:

30g (1oz) unsalted butter

Add the apples and cook, stirring frequently, until the apples release their juices and start to soften, about 5 minutes. Sprinkle with:

2 tbsp sugar

Stir to mix. Continue cooking the apples, turning them occasionally, until they have a light crust and are golden caramel in colour, 10 to 15 minutes. Use the apples immediately or cover and keep at room temperature for up to 2 hours. Reheat before using.

To assemble the crêpes, place a seasoned crêpe pan or frying pan over medium heat and coat it with a little:

Unsalted butter

One by one, add:

12 Basic Sweet Crêpes, *above*

Heat one side only in the hot pan for about 30 seconds. Fold the crêpe into quarters, so that it forms a ruffle-edged triangle with the brownest side out, and transfer it to a warmed plate. Arrange 2 crêpes on each plate so that they overlap each other slightly in the centre. Continue heating and arranging the crêpes, rubbing the pan with a little butter before heating each one. Divide the hot caramelized apples among the plates and spoon the warm syrup over all. Serve immediately as is or topped with:

Lightly sweetened whipped cream or *Crème Fraîche*, 87

STORING CRÊPES AND BLINTZES

Place the first crêpe or blintz on a plate and cover it with a square of greaseproof paper. Continue layering the crêpes between sheets of greaseproof paper. Cover the plate with cling film and refrigerate overnight or wrap airtight and freeze for up to 1 month.

Blintzes

About twelve 19-cm (7½-in) blintzes

Combine in a blender or food processor until smooth:

140g (5oz) plain flour
250ml (8floz) milk
3 large eggs
30g (1oz) unsalted butter, melted
2 tsp sugar
Pinch of salt

Pour the batter into a jug or other container with a pouring lip. Cover with cling film and let stand at room temperature for 30 minutes or refrigerate for up to 2 days.

Place a non-stick or seasoned crêpe pan over medium heat. Coat the pan with a little:

Unsalted butter

Stir the batter and pour 2½ to 3 tablespoons into the pan, lifting the pan off the heat and tilting and rotating it so that the batter forms an even layer. Cook until the top is dry and set and the underside is golden. Remove the blintz to a piece of greaseproof paper. Continue cooking the rest of the blintzes, buttering the pan and stirring the batter before starting each one. Stack the finished blintzes between sheets of grease-proof paper. Use as soon as they are cool enough to fill and roll, or let cool, wrap airtight, and freeze for up to 1 month.

Blueberry Blintzes

6 filled blintzes; 6 servings

Combine in a medium saucepan:

120g (4oz) fresh/frozen blueberries
Juice and finely grated zest of
    ½ lemon
2 tbsp sugar
½ tsp ground ginger
¼ tsp ground cinnamon

Bring to a boil over medium heat, stirring constantly, then continue to boil until most of the berries have popped and the mixture is the consistency of jam. Add:

120g (4oz) fresh/frozen blueberries

Cook and stir for 1 minute. Transfer to a bowl and let cool to room temperature. Spoon the filling in the centre of the uncooked side of:

6 Blintzes, above

Fold the sides of each blintz around the filling to form a rectangle. In a large, preferably non-stick, frying pan heat over medium heat:

30g (1oz) unsalted butter
1 tbsp vegetable oil

When the butter is melted and the bubbles subside, add the blintzes, seam side down, and cook until golden brown on both sides. Transfer the blintzes to paper towels to drain for a moment. Serve immediately with (opposite):

Lemon curd or topping of your
    choice

Sweet Cheese Blintzes

8 filled blintzes; 4 servings

Combine in a blender or food processor until smooth:

275g (10oz) curd cheese or
    drained small-curd cottage
    cheese
60g (2oz) cream cheese
1 large egg
1 tbsp sugar
1 tsp vanilla extract
¼ tsp salt
Grated zest of ½ orange (optional)

Transfer to a bowl and stir in:

75g (3oz) plump raisins (optional)

Spoon the filling in the centre of the uncooked side of:

8 Blintzes, above

Fold the sides of each blintz around the filling to form a rectangular package. (At this point, the filled blintzes can be wrapped airtight and frozen for up to 1 month.) In a large frying pan, preferably non-stick, heat over medium heat:

60g (2oz) unsalted butter
1 tbsp vegetable oil

When the butter is melted and the bubbles subside, add the blintzes, seam side down, and cook until golden brown on both sides. Transfer the blintzes to paper towels to drain for a moment. Serve immediately with:

Sour cream

Making Doughnuts and Beignets

The doughnut harks back to *Olie-Koechen* (Dutch "fried cake"), which was probably taken to America with Dutch settlers of the 1640s but may have arrived even earlier, with the Pilgrims, who spent several years in exile in Holland before making their way to Plymouth.

You can fry doughnuts in any oil or solid shortening. Most important, the fat must be impeccably fresh and clean. Using a deep frying pan, saucepan, or fryer – an electric deep fryer with a rotating basket is highly recommended – heat about 8cm (3in) of fat to a steady temperature of 180° to 187°C (360° to 370°F), unless otherwise specified. To keep the fat at a constant temperature, fry no more than 2 or 3 doughnuts at a time, being careful not to crowd them. The easiest way to slip a doughnut into fat is to dip a metal spatula into the hot fat and then lift the doughnut with the spatula from the counter into the pan, once again immersing the spatula. It is hard to give exact cooking times. Colour is a better indicator than the clock, so fry doughnuts until they are deeply golden on one side, then flip them over. When the doughnuts are done, remove them from the fryer with tongs or a long-tined fork and transfer them to a triple layer of paper towels to drain, patting off any excess fat. As soon as one doughnut comes out of the fryer, another should go in. If you like sugared doughnuts, shake them in a bag of granulated sugar while still warm or dust with icing sugar after they cool a bit. Doughnuts taste best while they are still warm.

HOW TO MIX AND CUT DOUGHNUTS

Like cake batters, doughnut doughs are best made with room-temperature ingredients. Handle the dough minimally and chill before rolling and cutting. When at high altitudes, yeast-based doughnuts require no adjustment; for quick-leavened doughnuts, reduce the baking powder or bicarbonate of soda by one-quarter but do not use less than ½ teaspoon bicarbonate of soda for each 250ml (9floz) if sour milk or sour cream is used.

1 The dough should be rolled or patted 6mm to 1.2cm (¼ to ½ in) thick.

2 Cut the dough with a well-floured doughnut cutter – a double cutter with a handle.

3 If that implement is unavailable, two biscuit cutters – one about 6 to 7.5cm (2½ to 3in) in diameter and the other about 2.5cm (1in) in diameter – will do as well.

4 Transfer the doughnuts to a piece of greaseproof paper and let them air-dry for about 10 minutes; the slight crust they will develop will reduce the amount of fat absorbed during frying.

Honey-Dipped Doughnuts

About twenty-four 7-cm (2¾-in) doughnuts

This easy dough behaves much like a brioche dough, meaning that it will fall apart as you mix it and then come together. It is important that after adding each egg the dough be beaten until it comes together and cleans the sides of the bowl.

Stir together in a medium bowl:

250ml (8floz) warm (40° to 46°C/ 105° to 115°F) water

4½ tsp active dry yeast

Let stand until the yeast is dissolved, about 5 minutes. Add and stir until the mixture is smooth:

140g (5oz) plain flour

Cover the bowl tightly with cling film and let rise in a warm place until bubbly, 30 to 60 minutes.

In a large bowl, beat until creamy, about 30 seconds:

140g (5oz) unsalted butter

Gradually add and beat until light and fluffy:

120g (4oz) sugar

Add, one at a time, beating for about 1 minute after each addition:

3 large eggs

Add and beat until blended:

2 tsp vanilla extract

1 tsp salt

Grated zest of ½ lemon or ¼ orange (optional)

Add the yeast mixture along with:

500g (17oz) plain flour

Mix until the flour is fully incorporated and the dough, which will be very soft and golden, wraps around the dough hook or paddle and comes away from the sides of the bowl. (If you do not have a heavy-duty mixer, the batter can be beaten by hand with a wooden spoon.) Butter a large bowl, add the dough, and turn it so that its entire surface is lightly coated with butter. Cover the bowl tightly with cling film and let rise in a warm place until doubled in volume, 1½ to 2 hours. Punch the dough down, wrap tightly in cling film and then a large plastic bag, and refrigerate for at least 3 hours or overnight. (The dough will rise a little and may pop out of its cling film, which is the reason for the large plastic bag. You don't want the dough to be exposed to the air and develop a crust.)

Working on a lightly floured surface with half of the dough at a time, pat or roll the dough out 1.2cm (½ in) thick. Cut with a well-floured doughnut cutter and place the doughnuts and holes on a sheet of greaseproof paper. Repeat with the remaining half of the dough. Let rise, uncovered, in a warm place until soft and puffy to the touch, about 30 minutes.

Drop the doughnuts and holes, 2 or 3 at a time, into deep fat heated to 185°C (365°F), opposite. Fry until golden on both sides. Drain well on paper towels.

Pour into a small saucepan to a depth of 5cm (2in):

Honey

Bring to a boil. As soon as the doughnuts are removed from the fryer and drained, poke a few holes in their sides with a cocktail stick. Place each doughnut in the boiling honey, count about 15 seconds, then turn it over and do the same to the second side. Transfer to a rack placed over a piece of greaseproof paper. Repeat with the remaining doughnuts, replenishing the honey as needed. Serve when the dip has dried.

Sour Cream Cake Doughnuts

About twelve 7-cm (2¾-in) doughnuts

These doughnuts have an inviting tang and a firm crumb that will recall your favourite sour cream coffee cake.

Whisk together in a medium bowl:

280g (10oz) plain flour
2½ tsp baking powder
½ tsp bicarbonate of soda
½ tsp salt
½ tsp ground cinnamon

In a large bowl, beat until foamy:

2 large eggs

Gradually add and beat until thoroughly blended:

95g (3½ oz) sugar

Stir in until blended:

125ml (4floz) sour cream
1 tsp vanilla extract

Add the dry ingredients and stir just until incorporated. The dough will be very soft. Pat the dough into a disk, wrap it in cling film, and refrigerate for at least 2 hours or up to 2 days. The dough will never become firm but it will be workable when cold.

Working on a lightly floured surface, pat or roll the dough out 1.2cm (½ in) thick. Cut with a well-floured doughnut cutter, keeping the doughnut holes too. Drop the doughnuts and holes, 2 or 3 at a time, into deep fat heated to 185° (365°F) (see page 68). Fry until golden on both sides. Drain well on paper towels and either dust with:

Icing sugar

or shake in a bag with:

Sugar or cinnamon and sugar

Serve while still warm or within a few hours of frying.

Buttermilk Potato Doughnuts

About thirty 7-cm (2¾-in) doughnuts

Potatoes passed through a ricer yield the most velvety doughnuts. Potatoes low in moisture and high in starch are described as mealy and are called baking potatoes. When cooked, their flesh is dry and fluffy, exactly right for baking and ricing.

Peel and cut into small cubes:

2 medium baking potatoes

Boil the potatoes in a large quantity of lightly salted water until they can be pierced easily with the point of a knife. Drain the potatoes very well, then push them through a ricer. Measure 190g (7oz) riced potatoes; keep any leftovers for another use.

Whisk together in a medium bowl:

525g (19oz) plain flour
2½ tsp baking powder
1 tsp salt
½ tsp bicarbonate of soda
¼ tsp freshly grated or ground nutmeg

In a large bowl, beat until foamy:

2 large eggs

Gradually add and beat until thoroughly blended:

120g (4oz) sugar

Stir in until blended:

250ml (8floz) buttermilk
60g (2oz) unsalted butter, melted
1 tsp vanilla extract

Stir in the riced potatoes. Add the dry ingredients and stir just until incorporated. The dough will be very soft. Pat the dough into a disk, wrap it in cling film, and refrigerate for at least 2 hours or up to 2 days. The dough will never become firm but it will be workable when cold. Working on a lightly floured surface with half of the dough at a time, pat or roll the dough out 1.2cm (½ in) thick. Cut with a well-floured doughnut cutter and place the doughnuts and holes on a sheet of greaseproof paper. Repeat with the remaining half of the dough. Drop the doughnuts and holes, 2 or 3 at a time, into deep fat heated to 185°C (365°F) (see page 68). Fry until golden on both sides. Drain well on paper towels and either dust with:

Icing sugar

or shake in a bag with:

Sugar

Serve while still warm or within a few hours of frying.

USING A POTATO RICER

A potato ricer is the best tool for preparing light, even-textured mashed potatoes. Look for a sturdy metal ricer with at least a 500ml (16floz) perforated bowl for holding the boiled potatoes and two long handles that, when squeezed, force the potatoes through holes in the bottom of the cup. A good ricer should come with two disks of different-sized perforations. Use smaller holes for finely riced potatoes.

Beignets

About 15 beignets

Beignets are a speciality of New Orleans, where they are traditionally served with chicory-flavoured coffee.
Combine in a medium saucepan and bring to a steady boil:

125ml (4floz) water
60g (2oz) unsalted butter
1 tbsp sugar
½ tsp salt

Add all at once:

70g (2½ oz) plain flour

Stir vigorously, without stopping, over medium heat until the mixture comes together and takes on a shine. Continue to cook, stirring constantly, for 2 minutes. When you remove the pan from the heat, you will notice that the flour has formed a light crust on the bottom of the pan. Transfer the mixture to a bowl. Add, one at a time, beating at a medium speed for 2 to 3 minutes after each addition and scraping down the sides of the bowl:

4 large eggs

The mixture should be smooth and shiny, and should fold over on itself in a ribbon when the beater is lifted. Beat in:

2 tsp vanilla extract

Immediately drop the dough, a scant tablespoon at a time, into deep fat heated to 185°C (365°F) (see page 68). Fry 4 or 5 beignets at a time until puffed and golden on both sides. Drain well on paper towels and dust with:

Icing sugar

ABOUT
GRAINS

*T*hey say love comes when you least expect it, and that's what's been happening with grains. People pampered their whole lives with rich breakfast foods are suddenly finding that what they really crave some mornings is homely oatmeal or granola or cornmeal mush.

The quest for low-fat, high-fibre fare led to a much closer look at grains, which provide complex carbohydrates, protein, a very small amount of fat, many of the B-complex vitamins, and an essential array of minerals. By eating the six to eleven servings daily of grains recommended in dietary guidelines, you can consume the recommended amount of protein found in one to three small portions of meat, without the saturated fat and with much more fibre.

Good health food shops and some supermarkets will stock more than a dozen distinct grains. You'll find separate discussions of how to select the most common breakfast and brunch varieties – oats, cornmeal and grits, and rice – on the following pages, along with recipes that range from simple and healthy to downright luxurious.

Unsweetened Dried Fruit and Nut Granola, 75

Old-Fashioned Rolled Oats with Raisins and Spices

625ml (1 pint)

This recipe and the following cooked cereal are made with the old-fashioned flavours of brown sugar and spices.

Bring to a boil in a medium saucepan:

500ml (16floz) water

Stir in until blended:

150g (5oz) rolled oats

50g (2oz) raisins

Pinch of salt

Reduce the heat and simmer, uncovered, for 10 minutes. Stir in:

1 tsp vanilla extract

½ tsp ground cinnamon

¼ tsp freshly grated or ground nutmeg

Top each serving with:

1 to 2 tbsp light or dark brown sugar or pure maple syrup

Oatmeal with Raisins and Spices

825ml (1 ⅓ pints)

Bring to a boil in a medium saucepan:

1 litre (1¾ pints) water

Stir in until blended:

100g (3½ oz) oatmeal

Cook, stirring, until the mixture is thickened, about 3 minutes. Reduce the heat and simmer, uncovered, for 20 minutes, stirring the bottom of the pan often to discourage sticking. Stir in:

50g (2oz) raisins

Pinch of salt

1 tsp vanilla extract

½ tsp ground cinnamon

¼ tsp freshly grated or ground nutmeg

Continue to simmer for 10 minutes.

Top each serving with:

1 to 2 tbsp light or dark brown sugar or pure maple syrup

OATS

Oats deserve attention for their nutritional value, especially for their fibre, half of which is the insoluble type that aids digestion and the other half the soluble type that lowers cholesterol.

All oats are milled to remove an inedible hull but, after that, may be either processed as oatmeal or steamed and rolled to hasten cooking and prolong their shelf life. Oat groats, which we know more commonly as oatmeal, contain enough fat to warrant refrigeration; because they are less processed, they yield a chewier cereal that is less likely to turn to mush. The more oats are steamed, rolled, and cut, the faster they cook and the softer they turn. The flavour benefits of mixing oats with other grains are evident in multigrain breads and several of the cereals and granolas that follow, for the oats bring a sweetness to the mix.

Oatmeal, the all-time favourite cooked cereal, is available as old-fashioned rolled, quick cooking, and, of course, instant.

Muesli

750ml (1¼ pints)

Muesli, also called Swiss oatmeal, was developed in the late nineteenth century by a Swiss physician for his patients. Treat it like a dry cereal and eat it warmed or at room temperature.

Stir together in a large bowl:

100g (3½ oz) rolled oats
250ml (8floz) boiling water

Let stand, covered, overnight. The next morning, stir in:

80g (3oz) raisins
30g (1oz) chopped walnuts or unblanched almonds
20g (¾ oz) flaked unsweetened dried coconut
60g (2oz) chopped dried apricots
1 tsp light brown sugar

Spoon into bowls. (If desired, the cereal can be warmed in a small saucepan before serving.) Pour over each serving:

Warmed milk or cream to taste

Three-Grain Apple Cinnamon Granola

1.5 litres (2½ pints)

Combining two or three grains in one dish yields a sum greater than its parts in mingled fragrances and textures. Dried apples and ground cinnamon add a slightly different flavour to this mixture of oats, barley, and rye.

Preheat the oven to 150°C (300°F) Gas 2. In a 33- x 23-cm (13- x 9-in) baking pan, combine:

200g (7oz) old-fashioned rolled oats
180g (6oz) rolled barley
180g (6oz) rolled rye

Bake, stirring frequently, until toasted, about 15 minutes. Stir in:

200g (7oz) chopped walnuts
60g (2oz) raw wheat germ
60g (2oz) unsalted hulled sunflower seeds

Bake for 10 minutes. Let cool slightly, then stir in:

125ml (4floz) soy flour or dried milk powder
1 tbsp ground cinnamon

Heat, stirring, until blended:

160ml (5½ floz) honey
125ml (4floz) vegetable oil
1½ tsp vanilla extract

Add to the dry ingredients and stir until well coated.

Bake, stirring frequently, for 10 minutes. Stir in:

200g (7oz) chopped dried apples
80g (3oz) raisins

Cool. Store in an airtight container at room temperature for up to 5 days or up to 1 month in the refrigerator.

Unsweetened Dried Fruit and Nut Granola

1.5 litres (2½ pints)

No sugar or sweetener is added to this otherwise classic recipe for granola with dried fruits and nuts. Wheat germ contains almost as much fibre as wheat bran and more vitamins and minerals. Consider adding a teaspoon or two per serving of toasted wheat germ to any breakfast cereal. Serve the granola spooned over natural yogurt along with fresh fruit or eat it as a cold cereal.

Preheat the oven to 150°C (300°F) Gas 2.

Pour into a 33- x 23-cm (13- x 9-in) baking tray:

125ml (4floz) vegetable oil

Heat in the oven for about 10 minutes. Stir in:

200g (7oz) rolled oats
180g (6oz) wheat flakes
180g (6oz) rolled rye

Bake, stirring often, until toasted, about 15 minutes. Stir in:

100g (3½ oz) chopped walnuts, unblanched almonds, or hazelnuts
60g (2oz) unsalted hulled sunflower seeds
60g (2oz) raw wheat germ
2 tbsp sesame seeds

Bake, stirring once or twice, until toasted, about 10 minutes. Stir in:

160g (5½ oz) raisins
115g (4oz) chopped dried apricots or other dried fruit

Cool. Store in an airtight container at room temperature for up to 5 days or up to 1 month in the refrigerator.

Custard-Topped Spoon Bread

8 servings

In the oven, this quick and easy batter is transformed into moist corn bread topped with a layer of golden-crusted creamy custard. Serve it with bacon or sausage for breakfast, or even all alone – but try this luxurious dish at least once with pure maple syrup.

Place a rack in the lower third of the oven. Preheat to 180°C (350°F) Gas 4. Place an ungreased 20- x 20-cm (8- x 8-in) baking dish in the oven to heat. Whisk together thoroughly:

140g (5oz) plain flour
120g (4oz) cornmeal, preferably stone-ground

1 tsp baking powder
½ tsp bicarbonate of soda

Whisk together in a large bowl:

2 large eggs, lightly beaten
500ml (16floz) milk
60g (2oz) warm melted unsalted butter
2 tbsp sugar
1½ tbsp white vinegar
½ tsp salt

Add the dry ingredients to the wet ingredients and stir just until the batter is smooth and free of lumps. Add to the heated baking dish and tilt to coat the bottom:

15g (½ oz) butter, softened or melted

Scrape the batter into the baking dish and spread evenly. Set the dish on the oven rack. Pour over the batter slowly, without stirring:

250ml (8floz) whipping or double cream

Bake until the custard layer on top is puffed and golden brown but still quivery and a knife inserted in the centre comes out clean, 45 to 50 minutes. Remove from the oven and let stand for about 10 minutes before serving. Serve hot or warm.

Baked Cheese Grits

4 servings

Grits are a favourite dish throughout the American South, where they were eaten by Native Americans long before the colonists arrived. They can be cooked plain and served straight from the pot, eaten (like pasta or polenta) with any number of toppings, or enriched with butter, onions, garlic, and cheese and baked in a casserole, as they are here. We like to use Cheddar cheese, but you could use Parmesan or a combination of the two.

Bring to a boil in a large saucepan:

1.25 litres (2 pints) water

Meanwhile, melt in a small skillet over medium heat:

60g (2oz) butter

Add and cook, stirring, about 5 minutes, until translucent:

60g (2oz) chopped onions

Stir in and cook for 1 minute more:

1 clove garlic, finely chopped

Remove from the heat. Stir into the boiling water:

175g (6oz) grits

1 tsp salt

Cover and cook, stirring occasionally, over low heat until thickened, about 20 minutes.

Preheat the oven to 180°C (350°F) Gas 4. Butter a 2-litre (3-pint) casserole or soufflé dish.

Add the onion mixture to the grits along with:

200g (7oz) grated Cheddar cheese

Whisk together until blended:

125ml (4floz) milk

2 large eggs

¼ tsp ground red pepper

Gradually stir into the grits. Transfer to the casserole. Bake until a cocktail stick inserted in the centre comes out clean, 50 to 60 minutes.

SOUFFLÉED CHEESE GRITS

Prepare *Baked Cheese Grits, above,* substituting 2 large egg whites for the eggs. Beat the egg whites until soft peaks form, then fold into the grits just before spooning into the casserole. Bake as directed.

Cornmeal Mush

About 1 litre (1½ pints); 4 servings

Stir together in the top of a double boiler:

175g (6oz) white or yellow cornmeal

125ml (4floz) cold water

1 tsp salt, or to taste

Gradually stir in:

1 litre (1½ pints) boiling water, or half boiling water and half boiling milk

Stir until smooth. Place directly over the heat and cook, stirring, until the mixture boils, about 2 minutes. Place the top of the double boiler over boiling water. Cover and cook, stirring often, for 25 to 30 minutes. Spoon into bowls and drizzle over:

Melted butter

Molasses, pure maple syrup, sorghum, or honey

CORNMEAL AND GRITS

Corn on the cob previews the subtle sweetness of dried corn in all its forms. The very sweetest dried corn comes from the same ears sold as fresh, but we have not seen it sold outside Pennsylvania Dutch farm areas, where the kernels are rehydrated as stewed or creamed corn. The corn raised for drying and milling and sold as cornmeal, hominy, and grits is starchier and much less sugary; yet its flavour recalls the opulence of a cornfield ripe for harvest.

Dried corn is processed for hot breakfast cereal and side dishes in two basic ways. If it is simply ground, the product is cornmeal, and coarse, medium, or fine grind can be used in any recipe unless otherwise specified. If you buy stone-ground cornmeal, you are getting the oily germ with the starchy endosperm; the product has a higher fibre and mineral content, and it must be refrigerated. The more commonly available enriched degerminated cornmeal has lost its germ and thus has a more stable shelf life.

Made with either white or yellow cornmeal, cornmeal mush is a favourite breakfast food served with butter, molasses, sorghum, maple syrup, or honey. Buy cornmeal in amounts you can use within 1 month and store cornmeal in tightly covered jars in the pantry or refrigerate for up to 2 months.

Kedgeree

4 servings

A relative of the Indian khichri, a dish made of rice, lentils, and spices. The English, it seems, substituted smoked fish for lentils and added chopped egg.

Bring to a boil in a medium saucepan:

250ml (8floz) whipping or double cream

Add:

¼ tsp cayenne

¼ tsp turmeric

½ tsp salt

Simmer for 2 minutes. Add and heat through:

450g (1lb) cooked long-grain rice, preferably basmati or jasmine

Cut on a diagonal into thin slices:

4 spring onions, whites and greens separated

Fold the spring onion whites into the rice mixture along with:

4 smoked trout fillets (about 225g/ 8oz total), at room temperature, broken into 2.5-cm (1-in) pieces

Remove the kedgeree to a 1.25-litre (2-pint) soufflé dish or casserole. Top with the spring onion greens and:

3 hard-boiled eggs, chopped

Or, butter the dish, pack with kedgeree, and unmould. Top with spring onion greens and the eggs.

Rice Pudding

6 servings

The all-time favourite made with long- or medium-grain rice. A kernel of long-grain rice is three to five times longer than it is wide; the cooked kernels are fluffy and separate easily. Medium-grain kernels are closer to oval in shape, less than twice as long as they are wide, and contain more amylopectin, a waxy starch molecule that makes the cooked rice denser and the kernels more apt to cohere.

Have ready a serving bowl or six 150- to 175-ml (5- to 6-floz) custard cups or ramekins.
Combine in a large, heavy saucepan:

125g (4oz) medium- or long-grain white rice
375ml (12floz) water
Heaping ¼ tsp salt

Bring to a simmer over medium-high heat, then reduce the heat to low, cover, and simmer until the water has been absorbed, about 15 minutes. Stir in:

1 litre (1½ pints) whole milk
95g (3½ oz) sugar

Cook, uncovered, over medium heat for 30 to 40 minutes, stirring frequently, especially towards the end of cooking. The pudding is done when the rice and milk have amalgamated into a thick porridge. Do not overcook, or the pudding will be solid instead of creamy once cooled. Remove from the heat, then stir in:

½ tsp vanilla extract

Turn into the bowl or cups, then press cling film directly onto the surface to prevent a skin. Serve warm, at room temperature, or cold. If you wish, sprinkle with:

Ground cinnamon

The pudding can be accompanied with:

Whipped cream or a fruit sauce

Swedish Rice Pudding

8 to 10 servings

One of the greatest of all rice puddings – like a mousse, yet also creamy.

Prepare and keep hot:

Rice Pudding, above

Whisk together thoroughly:

2 large eggs
60g (2oz) sugar

Gradually stir 500ml (16floz) of the hot pudding into the eggs, then stir the mixture back into the remaining pudding. Cook, stirring constantly, over the lowest possible heat just until it begins to thicken, 3 to 5 minutes. Do not allow the pudding to simmer, or the eggs will turn slightly grainy. Immediately turn the pudding into a serving bowl, then press cling film directly onto the surface to prevent a skin forming. Refrigerate until cold.
Whip until stiff peaks form:

250ml (8floz) cold whipping or double cream

Gently fold the whipped cream into the cold pudding. Serve at once or refrigerate for up to 2 days. Spoon into bowls or goblets. If you wish, sprinkle with:

40g (1½ oz) chopped toasted almonds or hazelnuts

This is lovely when drizzled with:

Fresh Raspberry Sauce, 92

ABOUT **FRUITS** & FRUIT SAUCES

*F*ruits are pure pleasure – when they are ripe. Vitamins, minerals, and fibres have no more persuasive salesman than a juicy, honey-sweet peach. Eating fruit is good for everyone, of course: every fruit, like every vegetable, contains all vitamins (except B_{12} which is found in any dairy product), minerals, and phytochemicals – those nutrients whose health-promoting properties are forever being newly discovered.

As always, the best advice is to eat the most fresh fruit you can, and preferably to eat fruit that is local, in season, and perfectly ripe. The recipes in this chapter demonstrate how easy it is to follow that advice by serving fruit at breakfast or brunch.

Fresh Fruit Salad, 83

Shopping for Fresh Fruits

Most of the fruits in these pages can be found at a market – if not the supermarket, then a speciality food shop or ethnic market. As much as possible, buy fruits in their domestic season, and buy fruits for canning, freezing, and preserving at the peak of the season. Produce is most reasonable in price when plentiful, nutrition is greatest when fruits have not travelled for long, and flavour is richest when fruits reach the peak of their reproductive cycle. In the summer and early autumn, farmers' markets and roadside stands offer the greatest variety and generally the most flavourful selection. When, in cold weather, it is back to the supermarket, make friends with the produce manager so that when you want to sample a fruit before buying it, he or she will readily give you a taste.

The way to shop for fruits is not to make a list at home but to wait until you get to the shop and see and smell what is best. This is especially true when composing a fruit mixture.

RULES FOR FRUITS

• When possible, buy fruit grown organically. Select domestically raised fruit in its season. Fruit raised in your region is even better because nutrition is greatest when fruits have not travelled for long.

• Choose healthy-looking fruit – bright, plump, and sound. Become familiar with which fruits have been waxed or sprayed and urge the produce manager to provide unwaxed, unsprayed fruits.

• Do not wash fruit until serving time, then wash especially well any commercially raised fruits or fruits you suspect have been sprayed.

• To Ripen Fruit: Underripe fruits can be ripened most efficiently in a brown paper bag. Do not crowd the fruits in the bag. Place the bag at room temperature out of the sun. Turn the bag over every day so fruits can ripen evenly. Adding an apple or a banana will speed the process because these fruits emit a harmless gas that enhances ripening.

• After ripening, most fruits keep best when stored in a perforated plastic bag in the refrigerator salad drawer. The exceptions – avocados, bananas, citrus fruits, pineapples, and melons – can be refrigerated, but their quality is best preserved in a dark, cool (10° to 18°C/50° to 65°F) place.

• Wherever you keep them, give fruits a quick check daily. When a piece shows any sign of spoilage – mould or softness or oozing – remove it. Spoilage is infectious and will quickly ruin surrounding fruits.

• Peeling Fruit: In general, do not peel fruit if you can avoid it. More often than not, the peel is a rich source of flavour, interesting texture, and valuable nutrients. However, in certain recipes or preparations, peeling is desirable. To peel fruits with loosely attached skin, dip them in boiling water for 20 to 60 seconds, transfer to a bowl of cold water to cool, then slip off the skin.

• To Keep Fruits from Darkening: When preparing fruits whose flesh turns brown upon exposure to air, rub surfaces with the cut edge of a citrus fruit – lemon, orange, mandarin, grapefruit, or lime. A quantity of fruit can be kept in a bowl of acidulated water – mix ½ to 1 tablespoon lemon juice or white vinegar into 1 litre (1½ pints) water – for up to 20 minutes.

• When cooking fruit, retain nutrients by cooking quickly and using as little liquid as possible. Save cooking liquids and blend some into your breakfast fruit juice.

• Because fruits are acidic, all tools and pans should be made of non-reactive materials – stainless steel, enamelled cast iron, or non-stick coated.

• Dried fruits such as raisins, currants, and dried cherries benefit by being plumped before being added to a recipe. Plump them by soaking in warmed or boiling spirits, fruit juice, or any liquid in the recipe they are to be used in for 10 to 15 minutes before use.

HOW TO SEGMENT CITRUS FRUITS

The only fussy preparation of citrus is segmenting the fruit for a salad or dessert. This takes not skill but time – and it is worth it. Without its tough bitter casing, the delicate citrus pulp sparkles – chefs call these sections supremes.

I Slice off the top and bottom of the round fruit, down to the flesh. Stand the fruit on a grooved cutting board (to catch juices) and use a serrated knife to cut off the rind in even slices. Trim away any remaining white membrane.

2 and 3 Free each segment by cutting down against the membrane on either side. Lift out the segment and remove any seeds. At this point, the segments can be sliced or chopped, if desired. Squeeze all the juice from the membranes into a bowl.

Fresh Fruit Salad

10 to 12 servings

You can be sure a mix of fresh fruits will be pleasing to guests when you base it on year-round favourites, then add bright colours and flavours from fruits of the season (good proportions are about 900g (2lb) foundation fruits and 675 to 900g (1½ to 2lb) seasonal fruits). To keep the mixture from looking like a hash, cut pieces in a variety of shapes, none smaller than bite-sized. Although the fruits should be served within a few hours, you can enjoy them for a day or two – citrus juices and honey will keep seasonal fruits from darkening.

Add the following ingredients in the order given to a large mixing bowl, stirring gently every once in a while:

2 sweet oranges, peeled, seeded, and cut into bite-sized chunks

Juice of 1 large lemon
80ml (3floz) mild honey, preferably orange blossom, or sugar
2 green eating apples, cored and cut into medium dice
1 large ripe pear, cored and cut into bite-sized chunks
1 large banana, thinly sliced
Add 3 or 4 seasonal fruits, about 225g (8oz) each. Choose from:
Kiwis, peeled, cut lengthwise in half, and sliced
Strawberries, hulled and quartered lengthwise
Whole raspberries or blueberries
Stoned sweet cherries
Melon or watermelon balls
Peaches, nectarines, apricots, or plums, stoned and sliced
Seedless red grapes, stemmed

MACÉDOINE OF FRESH FRUITS

A macédoine is a fresh fruit salad flavoured with spirits. Classic spirits for fruit are wines – dry, sweet, and fortified, plain brandy, fruit brandy, and liqueurs. A splash of good-quality plain brandy adds elegance to every fruit. But if there were to be one bottle in the cupboard for fruit, our choice would be maraschino. Clear cherry-flavoured maraschino liqueur is incomparable with mixed fruit. Prepare Fresh Fruit Salad, left, adding 125ml (4floz) maraschino liqueur or 80ml (3floz) orange liqueur with the honey or sugar. Cover and refrigerate for about 4 hours before serving.

Melon and Prosciutto

4 to 6 servings

The inspiration for combining wedges of melon and paper-thin slices of prosciutto just may have come from proximity. Some of Italy's finest cantaloupes are grown not far from where some of its finest Parma hams are cured. This is one of summer's most refreshing first courses.

Cut in half and scoop out the seeds from:

1 ripe cantaloupe or Crenshaw melon (about 1.35kg/3lb), cool but not chilled

Slice each half into 6 wedges and remove the rind. Place 2 or 3 wedges on each plate. Cut into wide strips:

225g (8oz) thinly sliced prosciutto or Serrano ham

Drape the ham over the slices – or wrap each piece of fruit in ham. Serve at once and pass the peppermill.

MELONS

Unless otherwise noted, summer is the peak season for dessert melons – melons that are not watermelons. If a melon has no fruity perfume at the smooth (the blossom) end, do not buy it (unless it is a casaba). There should be a slight softness at the blossom end. Choose melons that are heaviest for their size with no soft spots, mould, or cracks and no strong aroma indicating over-ripeness. If, when you gently shake a melon, seeds rattle, chances are the melon is too ripe.

The only melons that ripen slightly after picking are the smooth, or winter, group. "Smooth" describes the rind relative to other melons.

Honeydew (below left) and Santa Claus or Christmas melons have smooth rinds, but Canary and Crenshaw melons are slightly wrinkled, and casabas have distinct wrinkles. "Winter" indicates the melons take longer to ripen than others. They are ready in the autumn. The flavour of these melons is mild and their flesh pale – light orange in Crenshaw and green to white in the rest. Smooth melons are fragrant when ripe, except for casaba. Casabas are ripe when golden yellow. The stem end may be slightly greenish.

Cantaloupe (below centre), nutmeg, muskmelon, and Persian melons are in the "netted" group. Choose those in which the netting is pronounced and

the fragrance is as sweet as you expect the flavour to be. The flesh should be musky and orange. "True cantaloupes" have another shape. They have a smooth, hard rind and may be lightly fluted. Their orange, green, or pink flesh is intensely sweet and perfumed. The great French Charentais melon (below right) is the most prominent in this group. A small crack close to the stem indicates full ripeness.

Stunning fruits blended from all of the above are termed "tropical melons". Galia, Ha-Ogen, Passport, French Breakfast, as well as other exotically flavoured fruits are available mostly from the home garden.

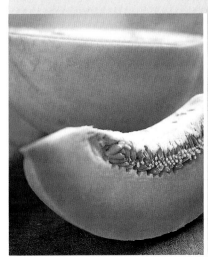

Grilled Grapefruit

4 servings

This delicious old-fashioned way with grapefruit can be served as a first course or for dessert. Pink grapefruit is preferred for its appealing colour. These can be prepared many hours in advance, then sugared and grilled just before serving.

Adjust the grill rack so the grapefruit will be about 10cm (4in) below a gas flame or 8cm (3in) below an electric element. Preheat the grill. Cut horizontally in half:

2 grapefruit, preferably pink

Remove any large seeds. If desired, snip out the tough centres. Loosen each section by cutting along the membranes and skin with a small serrated knife or grapefruit knife. Place the halves on a small rimmed baking sheet. Sprinkle with:

1 tbsp sugar

¼ tsp ground star anise or ground ginger (optional)

Leaving the grill door slightly ajar, grill the grapefruit until the tops begin to brown, about 5 minutes. Remove. For garnish, quickly place in the centre of each half:

1 small berry

Serve at once.

GRAPEFRUIT

White fleshed (pink) and pigmented (red) grapefruit can be found year-round. Select heavy, firm, round, or slightly flattened fruits with smooth skins. Those fruits with a brownish texture on the rind often have the best flavour. Avoid fruits with rough, puffy rinds. Marsh is the most popular white-fleshed grapefruit with few to no seeds. Star Ruby, Rio Red, and Flame are fruits of excellent quality with few to no seeds.

Apricot Compote

4 servings

When fruit is steeped in sugar, the sugar draws out its juice, forming a syrup. Here apricots are poached in their own syrup, brightened with orange. This results in a particularly rich apricot flavour. The skins toughen slightly in cooking.

If desired, peel by blanching:

10 sweet firm ripe apricots (550g/1¼ lb)

Cut each apricot in half along the seam line and remove the stone. Arrange cut sides up in a large shallow bowl. Spoon a little of the following into each cavity, in the order given:

60ml (2floz) fresh orange juice
45g (1½ oz) sugar

Cover and let stand in a cool place until the sugar is dissolved, about 2 hours. Turn the fruit cut sides down with their syrup into a heavy non-stick frying pan. Bring to a simmer over medium heat. Reduce the heat to low, cover, and cook until the apricots are tender when tested with a thin skewer, 7 to 8 minutes. They will continue cooking out of the pan, so do not overcook. Turn into a serving bowl cut sides up and pour the syrup over them. Cover and refrigerate for 1 hour, if desired. Serve warm or cool, sprinkled with (opposite, front):

Chopped pistachios or slivered almonds, toasted

Rhubarb Compote

3 servings

Botanically a vegetable, rhubarb has stalks that look like cherry-red celery but are less watery. Their flavour is tartness itself with a fruity aftertaste. Field-grown rhubarb is available principally in April and May; "forced" rhubarb, a paler pink colour, is available January to March.

Combine in a medium, heavy saucepan:

700g (1½ lb) 1-cm (½-in) pieces rhubarb
45 to 90g (1½ to 3oz) sugar

Let stand at room temperature until the rhubarb exudes some juice, at least 15 minutes. Bring the mixture to a boil over medium-high heat, stirring constantly. Reduce the heat to low, cover, and simmer, stirring occasionally, until the rhubarb is tender and the liquid thickened, 10 to 12 minutes. Remove from the heat and let cool without stirring. Refrigerate for at least 2 hours or for up to 2 days. The compote (opposite, rear) will thicken when chilled.

Prune Compote

6 servings

To stew plain prunes, omit the tea and orange juice. Cooked prunes will keep for at least 2 weeks in the refrigerator.

Combine with just enough water to cover in a medium, heavy saucepan:

450g (1lb) stoned prunes

Bring to a simmer. Reduce the heat to low, cover, and cook for 20 minutes. Gently stir in:

100g (3½ oz) sugar
125ml (4floz) fresh orange juice

Add:

2 bags Earl Grey tea

Cover and cook until all the prunes are tender, about 10 minutes more. Remove from the heat and refresh the flavour by blending in another:

125ml (4floz) fresh orange juice

Discard the tea bags and remove the fruit and syrup to a container. Cover tightly and refrigerate for at least 3 hours before serving – the compote will be best the next day. Accompany with:

Cream, *Crème Fraîche*, right, sour cream, or yogurt

Crème Fraîche

French crème fraîche results from a specific method of cream production that thickens the cream and gives it its characteristic nutty flavour. This crème fraîche is a delicious facsimile of the real thing. You can flavour it with vanilla extract and sweeten it lightly to taste, whip it and, generally, substitute it for double cream. If possible, avoid ultrapasteurized or sterilized cream.

Combine in a small saucepan and heat to 43°C (110°F).

250ml (8floz) double cream
1 tbsp buttermilk

Pour into a jar and keep in a warm place, loosely covered, until the cream is thickened and has a pleasant mildly sour flavour. This may take as little as 6 to 8 hours or as long as 3 days. Do not allow it to stand so long that the flavour becomes acidic or ammonia-like. (If you multiply the recipe, the culturing time may be longer.) Cover and refrigerate. The cream will thicken further when chilled. Crème fraîche keeps, refrigerated, for up to 3 weeks.

Apple Sauce

4 to 6 servings

This can be chunky or smooth. A blend of 2 or 3 apples makes the best-tasting sauce. Begin with a tart-sweet apple like Cox's Orange Pippin, then mix in spicy McIntosh with Gravensteins or winy Staymans with Pippins. Golden Delicious adds sunny sweetness to any blend.

Place in a large, heavy frying pan or saucepan:

1.35kg (3lb) cooking apples, peeled if desired, cored, cut into slices 1-cm (½-in) thick

125 to 175ml (4 to 6floz) fresh apple juice, depending on juiciness of apples

1 to 1½ tbsp fresh lemon juice, depending on tartness of apples

1 large cinnamon stick

Cover and simmer, stirring often, over low heat until tender but not mushy, about 20 minutes. Stir in:

Scant 100g (3½ oz) white or mus- covado sugar, or 6 tbsp mild honey

½ to 1 tsp ground ginger (optional)

½ tsp ground mace (optional)

½ tsp ground nutmeg

Cook, stirring, until the sweetener is dissolved and blended, about 1 minute. Remove from the heat.

Discard the cinnamon stick. For chunky apple sauce, break up the apples with a wooden spoon. For medium texture, crush with a potato masher. For smooth sauce, pass it through a food mill or coarse sieve. Serve warm or chilled. If desired, accompany with:

Double cream or yogurt

For a new flavour, sprinkle each serving with:

Anise or fennel seeds, toasted and crushed

Barbecued Bananas

4 servings

The banana is close to being the perfect fruit. It satisfies hunger pangs from the time its tips are green and its flesh is firm and faintly tart until its golden skin is speckled with brown and the fruit is creamy sweet. Select plump bananas with vibrant looking skin. If the skin looks dull, the fruit may have been damaged by cold and will not ripen. Ripen bananas out of the sun at room temperature, turning them daily.

Prepare a medium-hot charcoal fire. Peel and cut lengthwise in half:

4 ripe bananas

Cut each half on a diagonal into 3 pieces. Heat in a microwave oven or small saucepan until very fluid:

60ml (2 floz) honey

Toss the bananas with the honey in a shallow bowl until all are coated. This can be done 1 to 2 hours in advance.

Arrange the banana pieces crosswise on the rack over hot coals. Cook until marked on the bottom. Turn and cook just until the second side is marked. Arrange on a platter and dust lightly with:

Ground cinnamon

Ground ginger (optional)

Serve immediately.

These also can be pan-grilled in a ridged cast-iron frying pan. Heat the pan over high heat until very hot but not smoking. Quickly arrange about half the banana pieces crosswise on the ridges. Turn the pieces when they are marked on the bottom and remove them when marked on the second side, about 30 seconds to 1 minute each side. Repeat with the remaining bananas.

Apple Fritters

6 servings

Mix together in a medium bowl:

140g (5oz) plain flour

2 tbsp sugar

1½ tsp baking powder

¼ tsp salt

Whisk together in another bowl:

160ml (5 floz) milk

1 egg yolk

15g (½ oz) butter, melted

Gradually stir into the dry ingredients until smooth.

Pour into a shallow baking dish:

Juice of 1 lemon

Add and turn to coat:

4 large firm apples, peeled, cored, and cut into 6-mm (¼-in) slices

Pour into a deep fryer or deep, heavy saucepan and heat to 190° C (375°F):

8cm (3in) vegetable oil

Beat in a medium bowl until the peaks are stiff but not dry:

2 egg whites, at room temperature

Fold the egg whites into the batter. Working with a few apples at a time, shake off the lemon juice and dip them into the batter, letting the excess drip off. Immediately drop the slices into the hot oil and deep-fry, turning once, until golden brown and puffed. Drain the fritters on paper towels and keep warm in a 120°C (250°F) Gas ½ oven until all are finished. Serve the apple fritters sprinkled with:

Icing sugar or pure maple syrup

Baked Quinces

4 servings

Quinces can be difficult to core, but the results are worth it. The flesh may darken while you are preparing them, but the orange and apple juices will refresh their colour. These will keep in the refrigerator for several days. Serve with Ice Cream Mixed with Whipped Cream, *right.*

Preheat the oven to 150°C (300°F) Gas 2.

Thinly slice crosswise, then cut the slices in half:

1 large orange

Scrub off any fuzz and peel:

4 medium, ripe fragrant quinces (about 675g/1½ lb)

Halve and then quarter, using a large, heavy knife and slowly pushing the blade down through the fruit. Cut out the cores with a small serrated knife, catching all the gritty parts (save the trimmings for jelly). Arrange a layer of quinces cut sides up in a deep 2-litre (3-pint) baking dish. Sprinkle with:

1 tbsp sugar

Add a layer of orange slices. Continue layering to the top, finishing with orange slices. Add:

250ml (8floz) apple juice

Cover and bake until the quinces test tender when pierced with a thin skewer, 1½ to 3 hours. Remove from the oven and baste the top pieces with the juices. If the quinces are dry, cover them with more:

Apple juice (about 250ml/8floz)

Serve warm or chilled with the juices in the dish.

Ice Cream Mixed with Whipped Cream

6 servings

Whip until soft peaks form:

125ml (4floz) cold double or whipping cream

Cover and refrigerate for up to 2 hours.

Before serving, let stand at room temperature for 10 minutes:

500ml (16floz) vanilla ice cream

Mash the ice cream in a bowl and let stand until soft and fluffy but not soupy.

Fold the ice cream and whipped cream together until blended. Serve at once.

QUINCES

To fill a room with sweet, rich fragrance, place a ripe gold quince in the middle of it. A member of the rose family, a quince looks like a pear that grew fat and lumpy with a stubby neck. Probably because they are too astringent to eat raw, quinces have fallen out of favour. But when slices are cooked until translucent and a deep shade of red, their flavour is reminiscent of rose and apple, with a touch of pineapple in the variety called Pineapple quince. Not every variety of quince reddens when cooked; some turn gold. Quinces are available in October and November. They keep for up to 2 weeks in a perforated plastic bag in the refrigerator. Handle gently, for, surprisingly, these fruits bruise easily.

Roasted Nectarines with Raspberry Vinegar Glaze

4 servings

When baked at high heat, their skins turn russet.

Preheat the oven to 220°C (425°F) Gas 7.

With the tip of a knife, slash on 4 sides to stop the skin from bursting:

4 firm ripe nectarines

Place in a 23-cm (9-in) baking dish or tart tin and set the dish on a baking sheet. Combine in a saucepan:

250ml (8floz) raspberry vinegar
130g (4¼ oz) light brown sugar
30g (1oz) butter

Heat, stirring, over low heat until the sugar is dissolved and the butter melted. Pour over the nectarines.

Bake for 10 minutes and baste using a bulb baster. Bake for another 10 minutes, then turn the nectarines over with tongs. Bake until they test tender when pierced with a thin skewer, about 5 minutes more. Do not overcook. Carefully pour the glaze into a wide, heavy saucepan and boil it down until thickened, about 10 minutes. Loosely cover the nectarines with foil to keep warm. Stir into the glaze:

¼ tsp ground black pepper, or to taste

Pour over the nectarines in a serving dish and serve.

NECTARINES

Nectarines are peaches in plum clothing. They are a stone fruit. Look for nectarines in your local market in July and August. They do not have legendary varieties, and, even at their best, they are not as juicy as peaches, but their flavours can be sublime. If you substitute nectarines in a recipe for peaches, add a small amount of orange or pineapple juice to fill in for the missing juice. Nectarines are delicious, but they are impossible to halve and stone neatly.

Fresh Mango Sauce (Mango Coulis)

About 310ml (½ pint); 6 to 10 servings

An unusual sauce with a tropical accent.

Have ready:

1 large soft but not mushy mango

Stand the mango on a narrow side and slice the flesh free from either side of the stone. Using a paring knife, score the flesh of each half down to the skin in 1-cm (½-in) cubes. Push the skin inside out, popping up the mango dice and forming a mango "porcupine", then slice the flesh away from the skin. Peel the band of skin around the stone, then slice the flesh free and cut into chunks. Combine the mango in a blender or food processor with:

2 tbsp sugar

2 tbsp water

1 tbsp strained fresh lime or lemon juice

Purée until smooth. If the sauce is too thick, thin with a bit more water; if not sweet enough, add a little more sugar. Serve at once, or cover and refrigerate for up to 3 days.

Fresh Blueberry Sauce (Blueberry Coulis)

About 310ml (½ pint); 6 to 10 servings

Blueberries are sweet with enough tang to make them interesting – close your eyes and you taste plum. Blue on the outside and light green on the inside, cultivated berries are much larger than their wild forebears. The wild low-bush blueberries are small but intensely flavoured. Choose plump, round berries nicely covered with bloom, a whitish coating that preserves the moisture in blueberries and helps them keep longer than most other berries. Because blueberries are high in pectin, a jelling agent, this sauce will thicken upon standing. Whisk and thin, if necessary, with water.

Purée in a blender or food processor:

250g (8oz) blueberries, or 350g (12oz) frozen blueberries, thawed

3 tbsp sugar

1 tbsp strained fresh lemon juice

Strain through a fine-mesh sieve, pressing firmly with a rubber spatula. Taste, then stir in a little more sugar or lemon juice if needed. Serve at once, either at room temperature or chilled, or cover and refrigerate for up to 3 days.

Fresh Raspberry Sauce (Raspberry Coulis)

About 250ml (8floz); 6 to 8 servings

When perfectly ripe, a raspberry has an ambrosial flavour – sweet but tangy. Taste large raspberries before you buy them; they may be bland. Most raspberries are red, but yellow (or amber) raspberries are mutations from the red. Some yellow raspberries are delicious, but others are flavourless. Black or Blackcap raspberries are glossy purple black and almost round, very much like red raspberries but with a more pronounced flavour – and more seeds. They are excellent for all uses. Purple raspberries are a cross between black and red raspberries. They usually taste like tangy red raspberries. The straining of fresh raspberry sauce requires some patience. Use a flexible rubber spatula to push the pulp through a sieve. Press firmly and periodically scrape the inside of the sieve clear of seeds, which will otherwise plug up the holes. Do not waste the precious pulp. Continue to press until you are left with just a heaped tablespoon of stiff, clumped-together seeds.

Purée in a blender or food processor:

250g (8oz) raspberries, or 350g (12oz) frozen dry-pack raspberries, thawed

3 tbsp sugar

2 tsp strained fresh lemon juice

Strain through a fine-mesh sieve, pressing firmly with a rubber spatula. Taste, then stir in a little more sugar or lemon juice if needed. Serve at once, either at room temperature or chilled, or cover and refrigerate for up to 3 days.

Rich Hot Lemon Sauce

About 330ml (11floz); 6 to 10 servings

Similar to lemon curd but thinner, more transparent, and slightly sweeter, this sauce is traditional with gingerbread, pound cake, and angel cake. It is also delicious with dishes containing apples, blueberries, peaches, bananas, or coconut.

Combine in a small, heavy saucepan:

120g (4oz) sugar

60ml (2floz) strained fresh lemon juice

Grated zest of 1 lemon

2 tbsp water

Whisk in until thoroughly blended:

3 large egg yolks

Add:

115g (4oz) unsalted butter, cut into pieces

Set over low heat. Stirring constantly but gently with a heatproof rubber spatula or wooden spoon, bring the sauce to a simmer and cook until thickened, about 1 minute. Strain through a fine-mesh sieve. Serve at once, or let cool then cover and refrigerate for up to 3 days. Reheat over low heat or over hot water.

Hot Blueberry Sauce

About 500ml (16floz); 6 to 8 servings

Lovely over pound cake, hot scones, or corn bread.

Combine in a stainless-steel frying pan:

250g (8oz) blueberries, or 350g (12oz) frozen blueberries, frozen or thawed

60g (2oz) sugar

3 tbsp strained fresh lemon juice

Cook over medium-high heat, stirring, until the berries soften and release their juice. Stir to a smooth paste:

1 tbsp water

1½ tsp cornflour

Briskly stir the cornflour mixture into the berries and cook until thickened, about 1 minute. If using the sauce with a warm or room-temperature food, stir in:

15 to 30g (½ to 1oz) unsalted butter (optional)

Serve at once, or let cool then cover and refrigerate for up to 3 days. Reheat over low heat.

UNCOOKED FRUIT SAUCES (COULIS)

Strained purées of uncooked berries and other fruits are often called today by the French name *coulis*, which means strained juice. Whatever their name, these are lovely sauces, fresh in flavour and vivid in colour. Another bonus is that uncooked fruit sauces are very easy to make. Frozen fruit works as well as fresh, but be sure to use so-called dry-pack frozen fruit, which usually comes in a plastic bag, not fruit that has been prepared with a syrup. For an elegant, restaurant-style presentation, prepare two or more fresh fruit sauces in contrasting colours and spoon them in a decorative pattern onto large white plates.

ABOUT
COBBLERS,
CRISPS &
GALETTES

*W*ho says you can't eat dessert in the morning? As the recipes in this chapter show, some of the most homey of desserts are perfectly suited to serve for breakfast or brunch.

We love the names Americans have given their fruit-and-dough desserts over the years – pandowdy, cobbler, crisp, brown betty, crunch, slump, grunt, buckle. These desserts seem descended from puddings on one side and pies on the other. They may be based on scone dough, pie dough, dumplings, breadcrumbs, a crumbled flour-based topping, or cake; the fruit may be cooked under, over, or inside the dough or between dough layers. However they are made, these are plain, uncomplicated desserts – almost folklore, passed down from one generation to the next – made with whatever ingredients are available.

All these desserts are best freshly made or the morning after. Reheat them in the oven if needed, as the microwave steams and destroys a crisp topping. Serve them at the end of a gala brunch, or enjoy as a simple morning meal in itself with a cup of freshly brewed coffee or tea.

From front to back: *Half-Covered Peach Galette, 100; Half-Covered Berry Galette, 100*

Strawberry Rhubarb Cobbler

6 to 8 servings

An egg wash gives this cobbler topping a shiny, golden glaze when baked.

Position a rack in the lower third of the oven. Preheat the oven to 190°C (375°F) Gas 5. Have ready an unbuttered enamelled cast-iron, earthenware, or glass baking dish of about 2-litre (3-pint) capacity and 5cm (2in) deep, such as a 20- x 20-cm (8- x 8-in) or 28- x 17-cm (11- x 7-in) dish; a 30-cm (12-in) oval gratin; or a 23- x 5-cm (9- x 2-in) or 25- x 5-cm (10- x 2-in) glass pie dish.

Without peeling, cut into 2.5-cm (1-in) lengths:
550g (1¼ lb) rhubarb stalks
Place in a large bowl.
Wash and pat dry:
280g (10oz) strawberries
Hull and halve the berries; quarter if very large. Add them to the rhubarb. Stir together, then toss with the fruit:
100g (3½ oz) sugar
1 tbsp cornflour or 2 tbsp plain flour
Spread evenly in the baking dish.

Prepare:
Cornmeal Cobbler Biscuit Dough, opposite
Roll, pat out, shape into balls, or cut into desired shapes, as described. Brush with the glaze of your choice and sprinkle with:
Sugar
Arrange the dough over the fruit. Bake until the top is golden brown and the juices are bubbling, 45 to 50 minutes. Let cool for 15 minutes before serving. Serve with:
Softly whipped cream

Peach Raspberry Cobbler

6 to 8 servings

This cobbler has a cake-like batter that is spooned over the fruit. Buttermilk makes a flavourful and tender dough with less fat than usual. Bicarbonate of soda (instead of baking powder) works with the acidic buttermilk to give the batter lift. Peel the peaches if you like, but the skins add colour to the juices.

Position a rack in the lower third of the oven. Preheat the oven to 180°C (350°F) Gas 4. Have ready an unbuttered enamelled cast-iron, earthenware, or glass baking dish of about 2-litre (3-pint) capacity and 5cm (2in) deep, such as a 20- x 20-cm (8- x 8-in) or 28- x 17-cm (11- x 7-in) dish; a 30-cm (12-in) oval gratin; or a 23- x 5-cm (9- x 2-in) or 25- x 5-cm (10- x 2-in) glass pie dish.

Wash and wipe dry:

6 medium, ripe peaches (675 to 800g/1½ to 1¾ lb)

Cut in half and remove the stones. Cut each half into 5 wedges and spread evenly in the dish. Cover with:

250g (8oz) fresh or frozen raspberries

Sprinkle evenly over the top and set aside:

45g (1½ oz) sugar

Whisk together thoroughly:

140g (5oz) plain flour
1 tsp bicarbonate of soda
¼ tsp salt

In a separate bowl, beat until light and fluffy:

60g (2oz) unsalted butter, softened

60g (2oz) sugar

Beat in:

1 large egg

Add half of the dry ingredients and beat on low speed just until incorporated. Beat in:

60ml (2floz) buttermilk

Add the remaining dry ingredients and beat just until the batter is smooth. Drop spoonfuls of the batter on top of the fruit to cover it, leaving a 1-cm (½-in) border all around the edge of the dish to leave room for expansion during cooking. Bake until the top is golden brown and the fruit is tender when pierced, 40 to 45 minutes. Let cool for 15 minutes before serving. Serve with:

Softly whipped cream

Cornmeal Cobbler Biscuit Dough

1 cobbler topping

This recipe makes the perfect amount of dough for one cobbler recipe and may be varied with other ingredients, such as sour cream. While double cream makes the richest cobbler biscuit dough, milk is a fine substitute.

Have ready an unbuttered enamelled cast-iron, earthenware, or glass baking dish of about 2-litre (3-pint) capacity and 5cm (2in) deep, such as a 20- x 20-cm (8- x 8-in) or 28- x 17-cm (11- x 7-in) dish; a 30-cm (12-in) oval gratin; or a 23- x 5-cm (9- x 2-in) or 25- x 5-cm (10- x 2-in) glass pie dish. Whisk together in a bowl:

140g (5oz) plain flour
60g (2oz) cornmeal
2 tbsp sugar
1½ tsp baking powder

½ tsp salt

Add:

75g (2½ oz) cold unsalted butter, cut into small pieces

Toss with the dry ingredients. Using a pastry blender or 2 knives, cut the butter into the dry ingredients until the mixture resembles coarse crumbs. Add:

160ml (5floz) double cream or
125ml (4floz) milk

Mix with a wooden spoon, rubber spatula, or fork only until the dough comes together and can be rolled or patted. Gently knead the dough in the bowl 5 to 10 times if needed, turning and pressing any loose pieces into the dough. Dust the top and bottom of the dough with a little flour, then roll the dough to the shape of the top of the baking dish, 6mm to 1.2cm (¼ to ½ in) thick. Cut the dough into circles, squares, rectangles, or pie wedges, into 2.5-cm (1-in) strips for a lattice (lay the strips in opposite directions, weaving them if you like), or trim the edges and leave it whole. You may also roll small pieces into balls, flatten each one slightly, and place on the fruit. If leaving the dough whole, cut 3 small steam vents. Place the biscuit dough on the fruit. Lightly brush the top with:

15 to 30g (½ to 1oz) melted butter, or 1 to 2 tbsp cream, milk, or lightly beaten egg

Sprinkle with:

About 1 tbsp sugar

Bake the cobbler as directed in each recipe, typically 45 to 50 minutes.

Mango Pear Crisp

6 to 8 servings

Mango adds perfume and subtle background flavour to the pears, and crystallized ginger in the topping piques the taste buds with a little exotic heat. Bosc or Bartlett pears are the best choice for this dessert (opposite).

Position a rack in the lower third of the oven. Preheat the oven to 190°C (375°F) Gas 5. Have ready an unbuttered 2-litre (3-pint) earthenware or glass baking dish, 5cm (2 in) deep. Peel and core:

6 medium, firm ripe pears (about 900g/2lb)

Slice the pears in half and then each half into 4 wedges. Place in the baking dish. Peel and cut into 1-cm (½-in) slices:

2 slightly firm ripe mangoes (about 675g/1¼ lb)

Toss with the pears. Stir together:

100g (3½ oz) plain flour

100g (3½ oz) sugar
½ tsp salt
Add:
115g (4oz) cold unsalted butter, cut into small pieces

Using a pastry blender or 2 knives, cut the butter into the dry ingredients until the mixture resembles coarse crumbs. Or do this with a mixer or in a food processor, taking care not to blend the butter too thoroughly. Stir in:

45g (1½ oz) diced crystallized ginger

Scatter the topping evenly over the fruit. Tap the dish on the counter once or twice to settle in the crumbs. Bake until the topping is golden brown, the juices are bubbling, and the fruit is tender when pierced with a skewer, about 45 to 50 minutes. Serve warm.

PREPARING MANGOES

To cut up mangoes, cut the flesh from the long, broad, thin-edged stone. Score the skin lengthwise in quarters and pull off the peel. For an oval mango, hold it on one thin edge on a grooved cutting board. This will help catch the juice of the mango. With a sharp serrated knife, slice down either side of the stone, which is about 1cm (½ in) thick, removing two thick pieces. Cut the remaining flesh from the stone. Cut the flesh as desired. For a round mango, peel the same way. Then, working on one side at a time, cut the fruit down to the stone in slices or cubes, carefully slide the knife down underneath, and cut the pieces free of the stone. Repeat on the other side.

Raspberry Plum Crisp

6 to 8 servings

Frozen berries work well for this dessert, as long as they are not defrosted before baking. (Thawed berries cook too quickly and will turn to mush before the plums are sufficiently tender.) If you use frozen berries, increase the cooking time by 5 minutes.

Position a rack in the lower third of the oven. Preheat the oven to 190°C (375°F) Gas 5. Have ready an unbuttered 2-litre (3-pint) earthenware or glass baking dish, 5cm (2in) deep. Wash in cold water and dry:

8 to 10 medium to large ripe plums (about 1.1kg/2½ lb)

Cut in half and remove the stones. Cut the halves into 4 wedges and place in the baking dish. Sprinkle over the plums:

250g (8oz) fresh raspberries, or 175g (6oz) frozen raspberries
Stir together:
100g (3½ oz) plain flour
90g (3oz) light brown sugar
½ tsp salt
Add:
115g (4oz) cold unsalted butter, cut into 1-cm (½-in) slices
Toss with the dry ingredients. Using a pastry blender, cut the butter into

the dry ingredients until the mixture resembles coarse crumbs. Or do this with a mixer or in a food processor, taking care not to blend the butter too thoroughly. Stir in:

75g (2½ oz) chopped pecans

Scatter the topping evenly over the fruit. Tap the dish on the counter once or twice to settle in the crumbs. Bake until the topping is golden brown, the juices are bubbling, and the plums are tender when pierced with a skewer, 45 to 50 minutes. Serve warm.

Apple Galette

8 servings

A galette consists of a flat crust of pastry or bread dough covered with sugar, pastry cream, or a thin layer of fruit.
Prepare:
Deluxe Short Crust Pastry Dough, opposite
Position a rack in the lower third of the oven. Preheat the oven to 220°C (425°F) Gas 7.
On a sheet of parchment paper or foil, roll the dough into a 28- to 31-cm (11- to 12-in) round. Transfer the paper with the dough to a baking sheet. Melt and cool to lukewarm:
45g (1½ oz) unsalted butter
Brush a thin coat of butter over the pastry, reserving the rest. Sprinkle the pastry with:
1 tbsp sugar
Peel, core, and slice 3mm (⅛ in) thick:
2 large firm apples, such as Golden Delicious

Leaving bare a 2.5-cm (1-in) border at the edge, arrange the apple slices in slightly overlapping concentric rings on the pastry. Fold the dough border over the edge of the apples. Brush or drizzle all but about 2 teaspoons of the remaining melted butter over the apples. Combine, then sprinkle over the apples:
3 tbsp sugar
⅛ tsp ground cinnamon
Bake until the pastry begins to colour, 15 to 20 minutes. Reduce the oven temperature to 180°C (350°F) Gas 4 and bake until the pastry is golden brown and sounds crisp when poked with a skewer, 20 to 30 minutes more. Set the tin on a rack, brush the apples with the remaining butter, and let cool. Serve warm or at room temperature. The galette is best served the day it is made.

Half-Covered Berry or Peach Galette

8 servings

Prepare:
Deluxe Short Crust Pastry Dough, opposite
Position a rack in the lower third of the oven. Preheat the oven to 200°C (400°F) Gas 6.
On a well-floured work surface, roll the dough into a 33-cm (13-in) round. Carefully slide a rimless baking sheet beneath the dough, letting the edges of the dough overhang the sides of the sheet. Leaving bare a 5- to 8-cm (2- to 3-in) border at the edge, arrange in the centre:
180g (6oz) blueberries, raspberries, or thinly sliced peeled peaches

Scatter evenly over the fruit:
2 tbsp sugar
15g (½ oz) cold unsalted butter, cut into small pieces
Fold the border of dough over the fruit, forming a pleated half cover, with the fruit exposed in the centre. Lightly brush the dough with:
Milk
Sprinkle with:
1 to 2 tsp sugar
Bake the galette until golden brown, 25 to 35 minutes. Let cool on a rack. Serve warm or at room temperature. The galette is best served the day it is made.

Deluxe Short Crust Pastry Dough (Pâte Brisée)

One 23-cm (9-in) pie crust or one 28- to 33-cm (11- to 13-in) galette crust

Well-made short crust pastry is a paradox—firm and crisp, but tender, light, and flaky. It derives its strength from gluten, a tough, web-like molecule that forms when flour is moistened with water and then handled during the mixing and rolling of the dough. For tenderness, pie pastry depends on fat. This dough is rich in fat and is thus soft and difficult to handle, but it yields a marvellously tender, flaky crust with a superb butter flavour. While it is possible to make this dough with butter only, a small amount of shortening makes it flakier without interfering with the buttery taste. Since this dough tends to puff out of shape during baking, you should not use it to make a crust with a tightly fluted or braided edge.

Using a rubber spatula, thoroughly mix in a large bowl:

175g (6oz) plain flour

½ tsp white sugar, or 1½ tsp icing sugar

½ tsp salt

Working quickly to prevent softening, cut into 6-mm (¼-in) pieces:

115g (4oz) cold unsalted butter

Add the butter to the dry ingredients. Using a pastry blender or 2 knives, chop the butter into pea-sized pieces. Add:

30g (1oz) solid vegetable oil

With a few quick swipes of the pastry blender, cut the fat into large chunks and distribute throughout the bowl. Continue to chop with the pastry blender until the mixture resembles coarse crumbs with some pea-sized pieces. Do not let the mixture soften and begin to clump; it must remain dry and powdery. Drizzle over the flour and fat mixture:

3 tbsp iced water

Cut with the blade side of the rubber spatula until the mixture looks evenly moistened and begins to form small balls. Press down on the dough with the flat side of the spatula. If the balls of dough stick together, you have added enough water; if they do not, drizzle over the top:

1 tbsp iced water

Cut in the water, then press with your hands until the dough coheres. The dough should look rough, not smooth. Press the dough into a round flat disk, and wrap tightly in cling film. Refrigerate for at least 30 minutes, preferably for several hours, or for up to 2 days before rolling. The dough can also be wrapped airtight and frozen for up to 6 months; thaw completely before rolling.

HOW TO ROLL OUT PASTRY DOUGH

Flour the work surface – lightly if you are an experienced pastry maker but a bit more generously if you are starting out. Excessive flouring toughens dough, but sticking is a disaster.

1 Place the dough in the centre of the floured surface and flour the dough as well. Exerting even pressure on the pin, roll the dough from the centre out in all directions, stopping just short of the edge.

2 In order to keep the dough in a circular shape, each stroke should be made in the opposite direction from the one that preceded it. You can do this by rotating the dough itself rather than moving the pin. Be sure to check the dough for sticking by periodically sliding your hand beneath it; strew a little flour on the work surface as necessary. Seal cracks and splits by pushing the dough together with your fingers. If the split reopens, your dough is probably too dry. Dab the edges of the split with cold water, overlap the edges slightly, and press with your fingertips, sprinkling a little flour over the repaired area if it feels moist and sticky. Roll the dough roughly 7 to 10cm (3 to 4in) wider than your tin.

ABOUT
QUICK BREADS,
MUFFINS &
COFFEE CAKES

Q uick breads are so called because they are quickly mixed and, with the absence of yeast, need no lengthy rising time before baking. Thus gratification is never delayed. These breads encompass not only sweet and savoury loaves to serve as mealtime accompaniments or teatime temptations in lieu of yeasted breads, but also corn breads with savoury fillings, sweet morning coffee cakes, muffins, tender biscuits, and fanciful flavoured scones.

So very easy to make, these delightful breads are literally a busy person's "rabbit from a hat", and can transform a simple meal. Fresh muffins will turn a cup of coffee into breakfast good enough for a guest, and a homemade scone at four o'clock will attract the envy of workmates. For more elaborate occasions, any home cook can enhance a table with an astonishing array of quick breads in remarkably short order. It should also be noted that any coffee cake, quick bread, or corn bread recipe can be made into muffins.

Blueberry Muffins, 104

103

Making Quick Breads

Most quick breads are mixed in one of three ways: the muffin method, creaming method, or scone method. The muffin method is the simplest. First, whisk the dry ingredients. Second, whisk the wet ingredients, including brown sugar. Then combine the wet and dry ingredients by mixing or folding briefly – just enough to moisten the dry ingredients. Do not mix or beat the batter until smooth. Overmixed batters yield tough, rubbery muffins and breads with uneven shapes.

The creaming method is done with an electric mixer. All ingredients must be at room temperature. The butter is beaten with the sugar until lightened in colour and texture. The eggs are beaten in, followed by the dry ingredients, alternating with the main liquid. Quick breads mixed this way are often richer and have a finer cake-like texture than other breads.

Most scones, some quick breads, and coffee cakes are mixed by the scone method. The dry ingredients are mixed thoroughly; then cold butter is cut into the flour before the wet ingredients are added.

Blueberry Muffins

12 muffins

Position a rack in the centre of the oven. Preheat the oven to 200°C (400°F) Gas 6. Grease a standard 12-muffin tin or line with paper cups. Whisk together thoroughly in a large bowl:

280g (10oz) plain flour
1 tbsp baking powder
½ tsp salt
¼ tsp ground nutmeg (optional)
Whisk together in another bowl:
2 large eggs
250ml (8 floz) milk or cream
130g (4½ oz) white or light brown sugar
60 to 115g (2 to 4oz) warm melted unsalted butter or 4 to 8 tbsp vegetable oil
1 tsp vanilla extract
Add to the flour mixture and mix together just until the dry ingredients are moistened. Do not overmix; the batter should not be smooth. Fold in:
180g (6oz) fresh or frozen blueberries
Divide the batter among the muffin cups. Sprinkle with:
Cinnamon
Sugar
Bake until a cocktail stick inserted in 1 or 2 of the muffins comes out clean, 12 to 15 minutes. Let cool for 2 to 3 minutes before removing from the tin. If not serving hot, let cool on a rack. Serve as soon as possible, preferably within a few hours of baking.

Bran Muffins

24 muffins

Position a rack in the centre of the oven. Preheat the oven to 200°C (400°F) Gas 6. Grease 2 standard 12-muffin tins or line with paper cups.
In a large bowl, combine and let stand for 15 minutes:
90g (3oz) wheat bran
250ml (8 floz) boiling water
Whisk together thoroughly in another bowl:
260g (9oz) wholewheat flour
70g (2½ oz) plain flour
2½ tsp bicarbonate of soda
½ tsp salt
Whisk into the bran mixture:
175g (6oz) honey
80ml (3 floz) light molasses
6 tbsp vegetable oil
50g (2oz) light brown sugar
1 tsp orange zest
Whisk in:
2 large eggs
Stir in:
210g (7½ oz) raisins
100g (3½ oz) chopped walnuts
Add the flour mixture and fold just until the dry ingredients are moistened. The batter will be thick and soupy. Divide the batter among the muffin cups. Bake until a cocktail stick inserted in 1 or 2 of the muffins comes out clean, 15 to 18 minutes. Let cool for 2 to 3 minutes before removing from the tins. If not serving hot, let cool on a rack.

Apple Walnut Muffins

12 muffins

These are tender, flavoursome muffins.
Position a rack in the centre of the oven. Preheat the oven to 200°C (400°F) Gas 6. Grease a standard 12-muffin tin or line with paper cups. Whisk together thoroughly:

210g (7½ oz) plain flour
2 tsp baking powder
1½ tsp ground cinnamon
1 tsp bicarbonate of soda
Scant ½ tsp salt

Whisk together in a large bowl:

2 large eggs
140g (5oz) sugar

Stir in and let stand for 10 minutes:

180g (6oz) coarsely grated or
finely chopped peeled apples
(about 2 medium), with juice

Stir in:

75g (2½ oz) warm melted unsalted
butter
50g (2oz) coarsely chopped
walnuts or pecans

Add the flour mixture and fold just until the dry ingredients are moistened. Do not overmix; the batter should not be smooth. Divide the batter among the muffin cups. Bake until a cocktail stick inserted in 1 or 2 of the muffins comes out clean, 14 to 16 minutes. Let cool for 2 to 3 minutes before removing from the tin. If not serving hot, let cool on a rack. Serve as soon as possible, preferably the day they are baked.

MUFFIN TINS

Muffin tins should be greased or lined with paper cups. In either case, grease the top surface of the tin if you are making giant muffins with mushrooming tops. Fill the muffin cups to any level you wish. The standard is about two-thirds full. Batter for 12 standard size will make 48 miniature muffins, but only 6 to 8 jumbo. Muffin tin sizes vary, and baking times vary with them: a mini muffin will take 10 to 12 minutes, a standard-sized muffin 15 to 18 minutes, and a jumbo muffin 22 to 25 minutes.

Classic Currant Scones

8 large or 12 small scones

Serve with Clotted Cream, below. Position a rack in the centre of the oven. Preheat the oven to 220°C (425°F) Gas 7. Have ready a large ungreased baking sheet. Whisk together thoroughly in a large bowl:

280g (10oz) plain flour
60g (2oz) sugar
1 tbsp baking powder
½ tsp salt

Drop in:

85g (3oz) cold unsalted butter, cut into pieces

Cut in the butter with 2 knives or a pastry blender, tossing the pieces with the flour mixture to coat and separate them as you work, until the largest pieces are the size of peas and the rest resemble coarse crumbs. Do not allow the butter to melt or form a paste with the flour. Stir in:

80g (3oz) dried currants or raisins

Whisk together, then add all at once:

1 large egg
125ml (4floz) double cream
1 tsp grated orange zest

Mix with a rubber spatula, wooden spoon, or fork just until the dry ingredients are moistened. Gather the dough into a ball and knead it gently against the sides and bottom of the bowl 5 to 10 times, turning and pressing any loose pieces into the dough each time until they adhere and the bowl is fairly clean. Transfer to a lightly floured surface and pat the dough into a 20-cm (8-in) round about 2cm (¾ in) thick. Cut into 8 or 12 wedges and place at least 1cm (½ in) apart on the baking sheet. Brush the tops with:

2 to 3 tsp cream or milk

If desired, sprinkle the tops with:

Cinnamon and sugar

Bake until the tops are golden brown, 12 to 15 minutes. Let cool on a rack or serve warm.

MAKING CLOTTED CREAM

Let fresh unpasteurized cream stand for 12 hours in cold weather or 6 hours in warm weather and then put on low heat until rings form on the surface but the cream does not boil. Store in a cold place for at least 12 hours. Skim the surface.

LEMON SCONES

Prepare *Classic Currant Scones, above,* substituting for the dried currants 40g (1½ oz) chopped candied lemon peel. Increase the sugar by 1 tablespoon and use 1 tablespoon grated lemon zest in place of the orange zest.

CREAM SCONES

Double cream provides both the fat and the liquid in this simplest of all scone recipes.
Prepare *Classic Currant Scones, above,* omitting the butter and egg and increasing the double cream to 310ml (½ pint).

Popovers

12 medium popovers

It is important to bake popovers until they are well browned and crusty, or they will collapse.

Have all ingredients at room temperature. Position a rack in the centre of the oven. Preheat the oven to 230°C (450°F) Gas 8. Grease a popover tin or standard 12-muffin tin.

Whisk together thoroughly in a large bowl:

140g (5oz) plain flour

½ tsp salt

Whisk together in another bowl:

2 large eggs

310ml (½ pint) milk

15g (½ oz) warm melted unsalted butter

Pour over the flour mixture and fold just until blended. A few small lumps may remain. Fill the cups two-thirds to three-quarters full. Fill any unfilled cups one-third full with water so that the pan does not burn. Bake for 15 minutes at 230°C (450°F) Gas 8, then reduce the oven temperature to 180°C (350°F) Gas 4 and bake for 20 minutes more, until well browned and crusty. Do not open the oven to check the popovers until the last 5 minutes to avoid deflating them. Remove from the oven, unmould onto a rack, and puncture the sides with a sharp knife to let steam escape. Serve immediately or return to the turned-off oven for up to 30 minutes for extra crispness.

CHEESE POPOVERS

8 large popovers

You can bake these in eight 175-ml (6-floz) ovenproof ramekins. Grease lightly and dust the cups with flour so that the batter will climb as it rises. Have ready 50g (2oz) grated Parmesan cheese or 50g (2oz) cream cheese or soft fresh goat's cheese cut into 8 cubes (1 for each popover). Divide half the Popovers, left, batter equally among the cups, filling them about one-third full. Divide the cheese among the cups and cover with the remaining batter. Bake as directed.

Buttermilk Scones

Twenty 5-cm (2-in) scones

Position a rack in the centre of the oven. Preheat the oven to 230°C (450°F) Gas 8. Have ready a large ungreased baking sheet.

Whisk together thoroughly in a large bowl:

280g (10oz) plain flour
2 tsp baking powder
½ tsp bicarbonate of soda
½ to ¾ tsp salt

Drop in:

70 to 85g (2½ to 3oz) cold
** unsalted butter, cut into pieces**

Cut in the butter with 2 knives or a pastry blender, tossing the pieces with the flour mixture to coat and separate them as you work. For scones with crunchy edges and a flaky, layered structure, continue to cut in the butter until the largest pieces are the size of peas and the rest resemble crumbs. For classic fluffy scones, continue to cut in the butter until the mixture resembles coarse crumbs. Do not allow the butter to melt or form a paste with the flour. Add all at once:

175ml (6floz) buttermilk

Mix with a rubber spatula, wooden spoon, or fork just until most of the dry ingredients are moistened. With a lightly floured hand, gather the dough into a ball and knead it gently against the sides and bottom of the bowl 5 to 10 times, turning and pressing any loose pieces into the dough each time until they adhere and the bowl is fairly clean.

To shape round scones: Transfer the dough to a lightly floured surface. With a lightly floured rolling pin or your fingers, roll out or pat the dough 1cm (½ in) thick. Cut out 4- to 5-cm (1¾- to 2-in) rounds with a drinking glass or biscuit cutter dipped in flour; push the cutter straight down into the dough and pull it out without twisting for scones that will rise evenly. You can reroll the scraps and cut additional scones (they are never as tender as the first-cut).

To shape square scones: Roll out the dough 1cm (½ in) thick (6 to 8mm/¼ to ⅜ in if cooking on a griddle) into a square or rectangle. Trim a fraction from the edges of the dough with a sharp knife before cutting into 5-cm (2-in) squares.

For browner tops, you can brush the biscuit tops with:

Milk or melted butter

Place the scones on a baking sheet at least 2.5cm (1in) apart for scones with crusty sides or close together for scones that are joined and remain soft on the sides. Bake until the scones are golden brown on the top and a deeper golden brown on the bottom, 10 to 12 minutes. Serve hot.

Jonnycakes

Ten 7.5-cm (3-in) pancakes; 4 servings

Jonnycakes are a form of corn pone, America's original corn bread, made with only cornmeal, water, and salt. These are extraordinary frying pan corn cakes, crusty, almost crackly, on the outside, moist and creamy within, like polenta. In Rhode Island, the centre of the modern jonnycake universe, jonnycakes are eaten with pure maple syrup or butter and jam.

Combine in a large bowl:

250g (8oz) stone-ground cornmeal
1 tsp salt
1 tsp sugar

Pour over slowly, stirring constantly to prevent lumps:

560ml (1 pint) boiling water

Set aside for 10 minutes. Set 2 very large frying pans over medium heat. (You can also use a medium-hot griddle, set to about 160°C/325°F.) Add to each pan:

15g (½ oz) butter

When the butter begins to colour, add the batter by 60-ml (2½-floz) cupfuls. The cakes should be thick (about 2cm/¾ in) and no more than 7.5cm (3in) across. Smooth the top lightly with your fingertips if necessary. Let cook at a quiet sizzle, without allowing the butter to become darker than a pale nut brown, until the underside is a very deep golden brown, 6 to 11 minutes. Cut into extremely thin pats:

15 to 20g (½ to ¾ oz) unsalted
** butter**

Lightly press 1 pat onto each jonnycake, flip with a spatula, and let cook on the other side until deep golden brown, 6 to 11 minutes more. Keep warm in a low oven. Repeat with the remaining batter.

Banana Bread

8 servings

Have all ingredients at room temperature. Position a rack in the lower third of the oven. Preheat the oven to 180°C (350°F) Gas 4. Grease a 21- x 11-cm (8½- x 4½-in) loaf tin. Whisk together thoroughly:

185g (6½ oz) plain flour
¾ tsp salt
½ tsp bicarbonate of soda
¼ tsp baking powder

In a large bowl, beat on high speed until lightened in colour and texture, 2 to 3 minutes:

75g (2½ oz) unsalted butter
120g (4oz) sugar

Beat in the flour mixture until blended and the consistency of brown sugar. Gradually beat in:

2 large eggs, lightly beaten

Fold in just until combined:

2 very ripe bananas, mashed
50g (2oz) coarsely chopped walnuts or pecans

Scrape the batter into the pan and spread evenly. Bake until a cocktail stick inserted in the centre comes out clean, 50 to 60 minutes. Let cool in the tin on a rack for 5 to 10 minutes before unmoulding to cool completely on the rack.

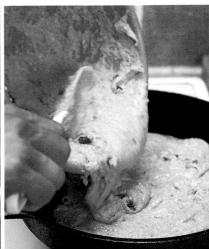

Buttermilk Crackling Corn Bread

8 servings

Preheat the oven to 220°C (425°F) Gas 7.

Rinse quickly, then pat dry:

115g (4oz) streaky bacon

Slice off and discard the rind, then cut the bacon into 6-mm (¼-in) dice. Turn into a heavy 23- or 25-cm (9- or 10-in) ovenproof frying pan, preferably cast iron, and cook over medium heat until very brown and crisp and the fat is rendered. Remove the pan from the heat.

Whisk together thoroughly in a large bowl:

120g (4oz) cornmeal
105g (4oz) plain flour
1½ tbsp baking powder
1 tbsp sugar (optional)
½ tsp bicarbonate of soda
½ tsp salt

Whisk until foamy in another bowl:

2 large eggs

Whisk in:

375ml (12floz) buttermilk

Add the wet ingredients to the dry and stir just until moistened. Fold the cracklings and all but 1 tablespoon of the fat into the pan. Set the pan over high heat until the fat smokes. Remove from the heat and pour in the batter all at once. Immediately set in the oven and bake until a cocktail stick inserted in the centre comes out clean, 15 to 25 minutes. Serve at once, either plain or with:

Jam or sorghum syrup

Deluxe Sunday Morning Coffee Cake

8 to 10 servings

Have all ingredients at room temperature. Position a rack in the centre of the oven. Preheat the oven to 180°C (350°F) Gas 4. Generously grease the bottom and lightly grease the sides of a 25-cm (10-in) springform tin. Sprinkle the bottom of the tin with:

Dry breadcrumbs

and turn lightly to coat. Tap out the excess crumbs.

In a large bowl, whisk together until well blended:

280g (10oz) plain flour
200g (7oz) sugar
1 tsp salt

Add and cut in with a whisk until the mixture resembles coarse crumbs:

140g (5oz) unsalted butter

Remove about one-third of the crumbs to a separate bowl and set aside. Add to the mixture remaining in the large bowl and whisk thoroughly:

1 tsp baking powder

½ tsp bicarbonate of soda

Add:

175ml (6floz) buttermilk or natural or low-fat yogurt
1 large egg
1 tsp vanilla extract

Whisk vigorously until the batter is smooth and fluffy, 1½ to 2 minutes. Scrape the batter into the prepared tin and smooth the top.

For the streusel topping, add to the reserved crumbs and toss with a fork until blended:

75g (2½ oz) walnuts or pecans, finely chopped
100g (3½ oz) dark brown sugar
1 tsp ground cinnamon

Sprinkle the crumbs over the batter. Bake until a wooden skewer inserted in the centre comes out clean, 50 to 65 minutes. Let cool in the tin on a rack for 5 to 10 minutes. Slide a slim knife around the cake to detach it from the tin. Remove the tin side. Let cool on the rack for 1½ hours before serving (opposite).

DELUXE RASPBERRY ALMOND COFFEE CAKE

This is a moist coffee cake. A portion of the dry ingredients becomes a streusel topping, while the rest is turned into a rich cake.

Prepare *Deluxe Sunday Morning Coffee Cake, left,* adding 1 teaspoon almond extract with the vanilla extract. Scrape the batter into the prepared tin and smooth the top. Stir 140g (5oz) seedless raspberry jam until smooth and fluid, then spread over the batter. For the streusel topping, omit the cinnamon and substitute 100g (3½ oz) sugar for the dark brown sugar and 110g (4oz) ground almonds for the chopped walnuts or pecans. Add 1 large egg yolk and 1 teaspoon almond extract and mix with a fork, then firmly knead the mixture with your fingers until the colour is uniform. Sprinkle the crumbs over the jam and bake as directed.

Sour Cream or Yogurt Coffee Cake

12 to 16 servings

Have all ingredients at room temperature. Position a rack in the lower third of the oven. Preheat the oven to 180°C (350°F) Gas 4. Grease a 33- x 23-cm (13- x 9-in) tin. Prepare and set aside:

Streusel topping, *Coffee Cake Loaf with Streusel,* 124

Whisk together thoroughly:

280g (10oz) plain flour
1 tsp baking powder
1 tsp bicarbonate of soda

½ tsp salt

Combine in another bowl and set aside:

310ml (½ pint) sour cream or yogurt
1 tsp vanilla extract

In a large bowl, beat on high speed until lightened in colour and texture, 3 to 4 minutes:

60g (2oz) unsalted butter
190g (6½ oz) sugar

Beat in 1 at a time:

2 large eggs

Add the flour mixture in 3 parts, alternating with the sour cream mixture in 2 parts, beating on low speed or stirring until smooth and scraping the sides of the bowl as necessary. Scrape the batter into the tin and spread evenly. Sprinkle with the streusel. Bake until a cocktail stick inserted in the centre comes out clean, 25 to 30 minutes. Cool briefly in the tin on a rack. Serve warm.

Old-Fashioned Gingerbread

8 servings

Dark, moist, and spicy.

Have all ingredients at toom temperature. Preheat the oven to 180°C (350°F) Gas 4. Grease and flour one 23- x 23-cm (9- x 9-in) tin or line the bottom with greaseproof or parchment paper.

Sift together:

295g (11oz) plain flour
1 tsp bicarbonate of soda
1 tbsp ground ginger
2 tsp ground cinnamon
¼ tsp ground cloves
¼ tsp salt

In a large bowl, beat until creamy, about 30 seconds:

115g (4oz) unsalted butter

Gradually add and beat on high speed until lightened in colour and texture, 2 to 3 minutes:

1 large egg
100g (3½ oz) light brown sugar

Gradually beat in:

250ml (8floz) light molasses

Add the flour mixture and stir just until combined. Stir in:

125ml (4floz) boiling water
3 tbsp finely chopped crystallized ginger (optional)

Scrape the batter into the tin. Bake until a cocktail stick inserted into the centre comes out clean, 35 to 40 minutes. Slide a thin knife around the cake to detach it from the tin. Invert the cake and peel off the paper liner, if using. Let cool right side up on the rack.

Apple Sauce Gingerbread

8 servings

This recipe contains no milk products.

Preheat the oven to 160°C (325°F) Gas 3. Grease and flour one 20- x 20-cm (8- x 8-in) tin or line the bottom with greaseproof or parchment paper. Bring to a boil in a medium saucepan:

250ml (8floz) apple sauce

Remove from the heat and stir in:

125ml (4floz) light molasses or golden syrup
1 tsp bicarbonate of soda

The mixture will foam and bubble vigorously. Let cool slightly. Meanwhile, sift together:

210g (7oz) plain flour
1 tsp ground ginger
¾ tsp ground cinnamon
¼ tsp ground cloves
¼ tsp salt

In a large bowl, beat on high speed until thick and pale yellow, 3 to 4 minutes:

2 large eggs
120g (4oz) sugar

Gradually beat in:

80ml (3floz) vegetable oil

Fold in the flour mixture in 3 parts, alternating with the apple sauce in 2 parts. Scrape the batter into the tin. Bake until a cocktail stick inserted into the centre comes out clean, 40 to 45 minutes. Let cool in the tin on a rack for 10 minutes. Slide a thin knife around the cake to detach it. Invert and peel off the paper liner, if using. Cool right side up on the rack.

GINGER

Mistakenly called a root, ginger is a tropical rhizome that is thought to be native to Southeast Asia. If it is fresh and firm, it will keep for a week or so sitting on the counter. To keep longer, put it into the salad drawer in the refrigerator, inside a perforated plastic bag with a paper towel to absorb any moisture. Select the hardest, heaviest rhizomes. Check where the knobs have been broken: the longer the rhizome has grown before harvesting, the more fibrous it becomes, and the more fibres you will see at the break. Mature fresh ginger is hotter and to some extent more flavoursome than young fresh ginger. Ground ginger, the indispensable spice for gingerbread, can be substituted for fresh, but is much hotter, so add it slowly as you taste.

Sour Cream Pound Cake Cockaigne

10 to 12 servings

A rich "plain cake" with a nuance of sour cream and a spectacular crackly brown top. Leftovers stay moist for close to a week.

Have all ingredients at room temperature. Preheat the oven to 160°C (325°F) Gas 3. Grease and flour one 23-cm (9-in) tube tin.

Sift together:

345g (12oz) sifted cake flour
¼ tsp bicarbonate of soda
¼ tsp salt

Combine:

250ml (8floz) sour cream
2 tsp vanilla extract

In a large bowl, beat until creamy, about 30 seconds:

225g (7½ oz) unsalted butter

Gradually add and beat on high speed until lightened in colour and texture, 3 to 5 minutes:

380g (14oz) sugar

Beat in 1 at a time:

6 large egg yolks

Add the flour mixture in 3 parts, alternating with the sour cream mixture in 2 parts, beating on low speed or stirring with a rubber spatula until smooth and scraping the sides of the bowl as necessary. In another large bowl, beat on medium speed until soft peaks form:

6 large egg whites
¼ tsp cream of tartar

Gradually add, beating on high speed:

100g (3½ oz) sugar

Beat until the peaks are stiff but not dry. Use a rubber spatula to fold one-quarter of the egg whites into the sour cream mixture, then fold in the remaining whites. Scrape the batter into the tin and spread evenly. Bake until a cocktail stick inserted into the centre comes out clean, 1 hour 10 minutes to 1 hour 20 minutes. Let cool in the tin on a rack for 10 minutes. Slide a thin knife around the cake to detach it from the tin. Invert the cake, then let cool right side up on the rack.

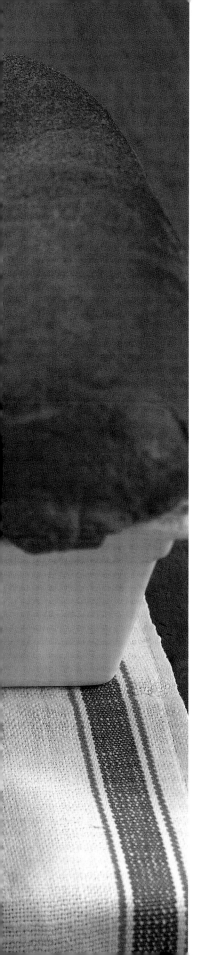

ABOUT **YEAST** BREADS

*W*aking up to the smell of freshly baked bread is one of life's most elemental pleasures. As the recipes in this chapter show, it can be possible to turn out home-baked bread for a special breakfast or brunch – or at the very least to bake bread the night before and have it ready to serve the next morning.

Yeast-risen bread dates back almost four thousand years to ancient Egypt, whose bakers discovered the secret of yeast, learned how to control it, and also developed ovens for baking several loaves at a time. In medieval England, the term for "dough kneader" developed gradually into the word "lady" – an indication of the respect, we have always thought justified, with which bread bakers have long been regarded.

The tradition of baking bread in the home kitchen nearly disappeared in Britain and America in the mid-twentieth century – and commercial loaves degenerated, for the most part, into sugar-dosed pre-sliced white bread. Many of us grew up never having tasted a home-baked loaf. The revival of professional interest in artisanal baking in the latter part of the century has spurred home cooks to try their hand at baking once again.

Cinnamon Raisin Loaf, 117

HOW TO KNEAD BREAD

Kneading converts flour, water, and leavening into a smooth and elastic bread dough, by developing the protein called gluten. Kneading may be done in an electric mixer with a dough hook or in a food processor, but because the process is so sensual and relaxing, many bakers prefer to knead by hand.

1 All doughs should be slightly sticky when first turned out from the mixing bowl onto the lightly floured board or kneading surface.

2 When kneading by hand, grease or flour your hands to prevent sticking, then work the dough with the heels of your hands, using firm pressure and pushing it against the work surface so the dough folds over itself as you work.

3 and 4 Continue in this way, pushing the dough away from yourself, peeling it off the surface, re-forming it into a loose ball, and giving it a quarter turn (use a pastry scraper to help turn the dough if it is supposed to be soft), for about 10 minutes, until the gluten has developed.

5 When finished, most doughs should be smooth and elastic, and tacky rather than sticky. To test, slowly and gently stretch a small piece of dough, turning it in a circular motion as you pull so that it stretches evenly. The dough should hold together without tearing until it forms a sheer membrane, thin enough to let light come through.

6 Alternately, you may simply test the temperature of the dough with an instant-read thermometer; the centre of the dough should register 25° to 26°C (77° to 80°F).

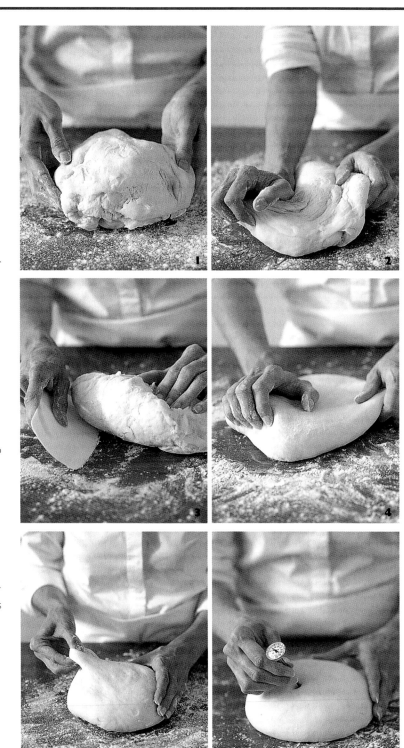

Cinnamon Raisin Loaf

One 21.5- x 11-cm (8½- x 4½-in) loaf

A favourite breakfast treat. The milk, egg, and butter impart a delicate rich flavour, tender crumb, and soft golden brown crust. The dough is also easily shaped into rolls.

Combine in a large mixing bowl or in the bowl of a heavy-duty mixer and let stand until the yeast is dissolved, about 5 minutes:

2¼ tsp active dry yeast

3 tbsp warm (40° to 46°C/105° to 115°F) water

Add:

250ml (8floz) whole or skimmed milk, warmed to 40° to 46°C (105° to 115°F)

65g (2½ oz) melted butter or margarine

3 tbsp sugar

1 large egg

1 tsp salt

Mix by hand or on low speed for 1 minute. Gradually stir in:

280g (10oz) strong bread flour

Gradually add until the dough is moist but not sticky:

210 to 280g (7 to 10oz) plain flour

Knead for about 10 minutes by hand or with the dough hook on low to medium speed until the dough is smooth and elastic. Transfer the dough to an oiled bowl and turn it over once to coat with oil. Cover loosely with cling film and let rise in a warm place (24° to 26°C 75° to 80°F) until doubled in volume, 1 to 1½ hours.

While the dough is rising, place in a small saucepan with enough cold water to cover by 1cm (½ in):

80g (3oz) raisins

Bring to a boil, drain well, and let cool. Stir together:

2 tbsp sugar

2 tsp ground cinnamon

Grease a 21.5- x 11-cm (8½- x 4½-in) loaf tin. Punch the dough down. Using a rolling pin, roll the dough into a rectangle 20-cm (8-in) wide, about 1cm (½ in) thick. Brush the surface of the dough with:

1½ tsp melted butter

Sprinkle all but 2 teaspoons of the cinnamon mixture over the dough, then spread the raisins evenly over the surface. Starting from one 20-cm (8-in) side, roll up the dough as you would a Swiss roll. Pinch the seam and ends closed. Place seam side down in the tin. Cover loosely with oiled cling film and let rise in a warm place until doubled in volume, 1 to 1½ hours.

Preheat the oven to 190°C (375°F) Gas 5. Whisk together and brush over the top of the loaf:

1 egg

Pinch of salt

Sprinkle the top of the dough with the remaining cinnamon mixture. Bake until the crust is deep golden brown and the bottom of the loaf sounds hollow when tapped, 40 to 45 minutes. Remove the loaf from the tin to a rack. While the bread is still hot, brush the top with:

2 tsp melted butter

Let cool completely before slicing.

KNEADING BY ELECTRIC MIXER OR FOOD PROCESSOR

When kneading by electric mixer, you will need a fairly powerful one with a dough hook, unless your dough is very wet. Make sure that the mixer bowl is large enough to hold the dough with room left over. Work the dough on low speed for about 3 minutes, until the dough is smooth and cleans the sides of the bowl. Continue to knead for about 7 minutes more. Knead the dough for a minute or two longer if necessary, but do not overdo it. Food processors mix and knead dough like lightning, in less than 2 minutes. Caution should be taken when using a food processor not to ruin a dough by overmixing. Plastic dough blades can mix and knead bread dough in less than 2 minutes. Larger machines will handle 840 to 980g (1¾ to 2¼ lb) flour for 2 loaves of bread. Some smaller machines will handle 420 to 490g (15 to 18oz) flour for 1 loaf of bread. (Be certain to check the machine's instructions before use to determine capacity).

Four-Strand Plaited Challah

1 braided loaf

This traditional Jewish Sabbath bread is a sort of butterless brioche. It is particularly good at breakfast time.

Combine in a large mixing bowl or the bowl of a heavy-duty mixer and let stand until the yeast is dissolved, about 5 minutes:

2¼ tsp active dry yeast

125ml (4floz) warm (40° to 46°C/ 105° to 115°F) water

Add:

70g (2½ oz) plain flour

2 large eggs, lightly beaten

2 egg yolks, lightly beaten

3 tbsp vegetable oil

3 tbsp sugar

1¼ tsp salt

Mix by hand or on low speed until thoroughly blended. Gradually stir in:

350g (12oz) strong bread flour

Knead for about 8 minutes by hand or with the dough hook on low to medium speed until the dough is smooth and elastic and no longer sticks to your hands or the bowl. Transfer the dough to an oiled bowl and turn it over once to coat with oil. Cover with cling film and let rise in a warm place (24° to 26°C/ 75° to 80°F) until doubled in volume, 1 to 1½ hours. Punch the dough down, knead briefly, and refrigerate covered until it has again nearly doubled in volume (a three-quarter rise is sufficient), 4 to 12 hours. The dough is now ready to be shaped. Weigh and divide the dough equally into 4 pieces. On an unfloured work surface, roll into balls and let rise, loosely covered with cling film, for 10 minutes. Grease a baking sheet and sprinkle it with:

Cornmeal

Roll the balls of dough into long ropes about 2.5cm (1in) thick and 50cm (20in) long, slightly tapering the ends. Dust the ropes of dough with:

Rye flour

so they will be distinctly separated. Arrange the 4 ropes side by side and pinch the top ends securely together. Plait the strips of dough in the following sequence, as shown opposite: Lift and place the fourth strand over the second. Lift and place the first strand over the third, then lift and place the second over the third. Repeat this sequence, placing the strand that is now the fourth over the second, the first over the third, then the second over the third. Continue plaiting until you reach the end of the strands. Pinch the bottom ends together and tuck both top and bottom ends underneath the plait. Set the loaf on the baking sheet. Whisk together and brush over the top of the loaf:

1 egg

Pinch of salt

Loosely cover the plait with lightly oiled cling film and let rise in a warm place until not quite doubled, about 45 minutes.

Preheat the oven to 190°C (375°F) Gas 5. Brush the loaf again with egg wash. If desired, sprinkle with:

1 tbsp poppy or
    sesame seeds

Bake until the crust is golden brown and the bottom of the loaf sounds hollow when tapped, 30 to 35 minutes. Let cool completely on a rack.

THREE-STRAND PLAITED CHALLAH

Anyone who has ever plaited hair or rope will have no trouble making challah plaits. You can divide the dough into as many strands as you like and plait accordingly, but this one is a simple three-strand challah plait, simpler to shape, in fact, than the four-strand plaited loaf above.

Prepare the dough for *Four-Strand Plaited Challah, above.* Weigh and divide the dough equally into 3 pieces. On an unfloured work surface, roll into balls and let rest, loosely covered with cling film, for 10 minutes. Grease a baking sheet and sprinkle it with cornmeal.

Roll each ball into a rope 33- to 36-cm (13- to 14-in) long, about 4cm (1½ in) thick and slightly tapered at the ends. Dust the 3 dough ropes with rye flour so they will be more distinctly separated. Place the 3 dough ropes side by side and pinch the top ends together. Lift the left dough rope and place it between the right and middle ropes. Lift the right rope and place it between the left and middle ropes, then the left rope between the right and middle ropes and so on until you reach the ends. Tuck both ends of the plait underneath the loaf and set it on the baking sheet. Finish as directed for *Four-Strand Plaited Challah.*

Hot Cross Buns

18 buns

Place in a small saucepan with just enough water to cover by 1cm (½ in):

80g (3oz) dried currants or raisins

Bring the water to a boil, then drain well. Transfer the currants to a small bowl and sprinkle with:

2 tbsp water

Cover and let soak at least 30 minutes. Stir together:

¼ tsp ground cinnamon

⅛ tsp freshly grated or ground nutmeg

⅛ tsp ground ginger

Prepare:

Cinnamon Raisin Loaf dough, 117

through the first rise, adding the spice mixture to the bread flour, and adding the drained currants towards the end of the kneading. Divide the dough equally into 18 pieces, about 30g (1oz) each. Grease a baking sheet. On an unfloured surface, roll the dough pieces into balls and place them 5cm (2in) apart on the baking sheet. For the egg wash, whisk together:

1 egg

Pinch of salt

Brush over the tops of the rolls. Cover with oiled cling film and let

rise in a warm place until doubled in volume, about 1 hour.

Preheat the oven to 220°C (425°F) Gas 7. Brush the rolls again with the egg wash. Bake the rolls until the crust is golden brown and the bottom sounds hollow when tapped, about 15 minutes. While the rolls are baking, make a glaze by stirring together:

90g (3oz) icing sugar

1 tbsp fresh lemon juice

While the rolls are still slightly warm, decorate each one with glaze in the shape of a cross (opposite).

Crumpets

12 crumpets

Muffin rings, real or improvised, are essential for making crumpets.

Warm to 40° to 46°C (105° to 115°F):

310ml (½ pint) water

310ml (½ pint) milk

Pour 60ml (2floz) of the milk mixture into a large bowl of a heavy-duty mixer. Sprinkle with:

2¼ tsp active dry yeast

Let stand until the yeast is dissolved, about 5 minutes. Add:

420g (15oz) plain flour

15g (½ oz) melted butter or margarine

1 tbsp sugar

1½ tsp salt

Mix by hand or on low speed while slowly pouring in the remaining milk mixture. Stir by hand for about 2 minutes or on medium speed for about 3 minutes. This is a very liquid, batter-like dough. Cover with cling film and let rise in a warm place

(24° to 26°C/75° to 80°F) until doubled in volume, about 1½ hours. Stir together until the bicarbonate of soda is dissolved:

1 tsp bicarbonate of soda

1 tbsp water

Stir the bicarbonate of soda mixture into the dough. Cover loosely with cling film and let rise in a warm place for 30 minutes. Heat a cast-iron frying pan or other heavy frying pan or griddle and add:

15g (½ oz) butter or margarine

Butter 9- to 10-cm (3½- to 4-in) muffin rings (or 225-g/8-oz pineapple tins with the tops and bottoms cleanly cut out).

When the pan is fairly hot, place the rings on the pan and spoon a scant 125ml (4floz) batter into each ring. Cook over medium-low heat until the batter rises and becomes bubbly on top and the underside is brown. Using a metal spatula, turn both the

ring and crumpet over. Remove the ring and cook the crumpet until the underside is golden brown, about 3 minutes longer. Remove to a rack to cool. When ready to eat, heat the crumpets in the oven or toast them. Serve with:

Butter or jam

STORING BREAD

Always let bread cool completely before wrapping it for storage. All loaves can be stored in cling film, though the crust will soften. Bread boxes and dry, cool, ventilated drawers or containers are also acceptable. Refrigeration tends to dry out bread, but well-wrapped loaves can be frozen for up to 3 months. Once thawed, however, they dry out more rapidly than freshly baked bread.

Kouglof (Kugelhopf)

I loaf

This slightly sweet decorative loaf comes from the Alsace region of France. Kouglof should be baked in a fluted ring mould. An earthenware mould is traditional, but metal or glass moulds work just as well. You can also use a plain tube or Bundt tin.

Place in a small saucepan with enough cold water to cover by 1cm (½ in):

80g (3oz) currants

Bring the water to a boil, then drain well. Transfer the currants to a small bowl and sprinkle with:

2 tbsp rum or water

Cover and let soak for at least 30 minutes or up to 3 days. Combine in a large mixing bowl or the bowl of a heavy-duty mixer and let stand until the yeast is dissolved, about 5 minutes:

2¼ tsp active dry yeast

125ml (4floz) whole milk, warmed to 40° to 46°C (105° to 115°F)

Add:

140g (5oz) plain flour

3 large eggs, lightly beaten

45g (1½ oz) sugar

1 tsp salt

Mix by hand or on low speed until blended. Gradually stir in:

250g (8oz) bread flour

Mix for about 3 minutes until all the ingredients are blended. Knead by hand for about 20 minutes or with the dough hook on low to medium speed for about 7 minutes. Because this is a rather sticky dough, hand kneading requires a particular technique: slap the dough down on the work surface, lift half of it upwards with both hands (part of it will remain stuck to the table, which is normal), and slap it down over onto itself. Repeat this until the dough is smooth and elastic and no longer sticky. Add:

140g (5oz) very soft butter

Vigorously knead in the butter until completely incorporated and the dough is once again smooth. Drain the soaked currants and knead them into the dough just enough to incorporate them. Place the dough in a buttered large bowl, cover with cling film, and let rise in a warm place (24° to 26°C/75° to 80°F) until doubled in volume, about 1½ hours.

Punch the dough down, knead briefly, and refrigerate, covered, for 4 to 12 hours. If the dough has doubled, punch it down and shape it. If it has not yet doubled, let it finish rising in a warm place, then punch it down and refrigerate for 30 minutes. Roll the dough on an unfloured work surface into a ball. Cover with cling film and let rest for 10 minutes. Butter a 1.75- to 2-litre (3 to 3¼-pint) kouglof mould or tube or Bundt tin. Sprinkle the bottom of the mould with:

30g (1oz) slivered almonds

Or place in the indentations in the bottom of the mould:

Whole almonds

Lightly dust the centre of the dough ball with flour. Make a small hole in the centre with your fingertips and gently stretch the dough to enlarge the hole just enough so that it fits around the tube in the centre of the mould. Place the dough ring in the mould, cover with cling film, and let rise in a warm place until doubled in volume, about 1 hour.

Preheat the oven to 190°C (375°F) Gas 5. Bake the kouglof until golden brown and a knife inserted in the middle of the loaf comes out clean, about 45 minutes. Immediately unmould the kouglof onto a rack. Dust the top with:

Icing sugar

Let cool completely. Just before serving, dust the top a second time with more:

Icing sugar

Coffee Cake Loaf with Streusel

One 23- x 12.5-cm (9- x 5-in) loaf

Combine in a large mixing bowl or the bowl of a heavy-duty mixer and let stand until the yeast is dissolved, about 5 minutes:

2¼ tsp active dry yeast
60ml (2floz) warm (40° to 46°C/105° to 115°F) water
Add:
70g (3oz) self-raising flour
60g (2oz) sugar
1 tsp salt
2 large eggs, lightly beaten
60ml (2floz) milk
1 tsp vanilla extract

Mix by hand or on low speed until blended. Gradually stir in:

280g (10oz) strong bread flour

Mix for 1 minute until the dough comes together. Knead by hand for about 10 minutes or with the dough hook on low to medium speed for 5 to 7 minutes until the dough is smooth and elastic and no longer sticks to your hands or the bowl. Add:

85g (3oz) very soft butter

Vigorously knead in the butter until completely incorporated and the dough is once again smooth. Place it in a large buttered bowl. Cover with cling film and let rise in a warm place (24° to 26°C/75° to 80°F) until doubled in volume, about 1½ hours. Punch down the dough, knead briefly, and refrigerate, covered, until doubled again, 4 to 12 hours. Punch down the dough and shape it. If it has not yet doubled, let the dough finish rising in a warm place, punch it down, and refrigerate for 30 minutes. Butter a 23- x 12.5-cm (9- x 5-in) loaf tin.

To make the streusel topping, blend with a fork or pulse in a food processor until the mixture resembles coarse crumbs:

90g (3½ oz) plain flour
80g (3oz) finely chopped walnuts
130g (4½ oz) light brown sugar
75g (2½ oz) unsalted butter, melted
1 tsp ground cinnamon
¼ tsp salt

Roll out the dough to a 30- x 23-cm (12- x 9-in) rectangle, about 8mm (⅓ in) thick. Brush the surface with:

1½ tsp melted butter
Sprinkle evenly with half the streusel topping along with:

35g (1½ oz) chopped walnuts (optional)

Starting from one short side, roll up the dough as you would a Swiss roll. Place seam side down in the loaf tin, cover loosely with cling film, and let rise in a warm place until doubled in volume, about 1½ hours. Preheat the oven to 190°C (375°F) Gas 5.

Whisk together and brush over the top of the loaf:

1 egg
Pinch of salt

Sprinkle the remaining streusel topping over the dough. Bake the loaf until golden brown and a knife inserted in the centre comes out clean, about 45 minutes. Unmould the loaf onto a rack and let cool.

Sticky Buns

8 buns

Prepare:
Coffee Cake Loaf with Streusel, above, through the first rise.
Butter a 33- x 23-cm (13- x 9-in) baking tin. Bring to a boil in a small saucepan over medium heat, stirring to dissolve the sugar:

200g (7oz) dark brown sugar
115g (4oz) butter
60ml (2½ floz) honey
Remove from the heat and stir in:
75g (2½ oz) chopped pecans (optional)

Pour the hot syrup into the baking tin and spread it evenly. Let cool. Roll out the dough to a 40- x 30-cm (16- x 12-in) rectangle. Brush with:

15g (½ oz) melted butter
Sprinkle with:
65g (2½ oz) dark brown sugar
2 tsp ground cinnamon
Starting from one long side, roll up the dough as you would a Swiss roll. Cut crosswise into 8 slices. Arrange the slices cut side down in the prepared tin, spacing the slices equally.

Cover the tin with cling film and let rise at room temperature until doubled in volume, about 1 hour. Preheat the oven to 180°C (350°F) Gas 4.
Bake until the buns are golden brown and the syrup is bubbling hot, about 30 minutes. Let the buns cool in the tin for 5 minutes, then invert the tin onto a baking sheet to collect the hot syrup. Serve warm or at room temperature, pulling the sticky buns (opposite) apart at the seams.

Index

Bold type indicates that a recipe has an accompanying photograph.

ACKNOWLEDGMENTS

Special thanks to my wife and editor in residence, Susan; our indispensable assistant and comrade, Mary Gilbert; and our friends and agents, Gene Winick and Sam Pinkus. Much appreciation also goes to Simon & Schuster, Scribner, and Weldon Owen for their devotion to this project. Thank you Carolyn, Susan, Bill, Marah, John, Terry, Roger, Gaye, Val, Norman, and all the other capable and talented folks who gave a part of themselves to the Joy of Cooking All About series.

My eternal appreciation goes to the food experts, writers, and editors whose contributions and collaborations are at the heart of Joy – especially Stephen Schmidt. He was to the 1997 edition what Chef Pierre Adrian was to Mom's final editions of Joy. Thank you one and all.

Ethan Becker

FOOD EXPERTS, WRITERS, AND EDITORS

Selma Abrams, Jody Adams, Samia Ahad, Bruce Aidells, Katherine Alford, Deirdre Allen, Pam Anderson, Elizabeth Andoh, Phillip Andres, Alice Arndt, John Ash, Nancy Baggett, Rick and Deann Bayless, Lee E. Benning, Rose Levy Beranbaum, Brigit Legere Binns, Jack Bishop, Carole Bloom, Arthur Boehm, Ed Brown, JeanMarie Brownson, Larry Catanzaro, Val Cipollone, Polly Clingerman, Elaine Corn, Bruce Cost, Amy Cotler, Brian Crawley, Gail Damerow, Linda Dann, Deirdre Davis, Jane Spencer Davis, Erica De Mane, Susan Derecskey, Abigail Johnson Dodge, Jim Dodge, Aurora Esther, Michele Fagerroos, Eva Forson, Margaret Fox, Betty Fussell, Mary Gilbert, Darra Goldstein, Elaine Gonzalez, Dorie Greenspan, Maria Guarnaschelli, Helen Gustafson, Pat Haley, Gordon Hamersley, Melissa Hamilton, Jessica Harris, Hallie Harron, Nao Hauser, William Hay, Larry Hayden, Kate Hays, Marcella Hazan, Tim Healea, Janie Hibler, Lee Hofstetter, Paula Hogan, Rosemary Howe, Mike Hughes, Jennifer Humphries, Dana Jacobi, Stephen Johnson, Lynne Rossetto Kasper, Denis Kelly, Fran Kennedy, Johanne Killeen and George Germon, Shirley King, Maya Klein, Diane M. Kochilas, Phyllis Kohn, Aglaia Kremezi, Mildred Kroll, Loni Kuhn, Corby Kummer, Virginia Lawrence, Jill Leigh, Karen Levin, Lori Longbotham, Susan Hermann Loomis, Emily Luchetti, Stephanie Lyness, Karen MacNeil, Deborah Madison, Linda Marino, Kathleen McAndrews, Alice Medrich, Anne Mendelson, Lisa Montenegro, Cindy Mushet, Marion Nestle, Toby Oksman, Joyce O'Neill, Suzen O'Rourke, Russ Parsons, Holly Pearson, James Peterson, Marina Petrakos, Mary Placek, Maricel Presilla, Marion K. Pruitt, Adam Rapoport, Mardee Haidin Regan, Peter Reinhart, Sarah Anne Reynolds, Madge Rosenberg, Nicole Routhier, Jon Rowley, Nancy Ross Ryan, Chris Schlesinger, Stephen Schmidt, Lisa Schumacher, Marie Simmons, Nina Simonds, A. Cort Sinnes, Sue Spitler, Marah Stets, Molly Stevens, Christopher Stoye, Susan Stuck, Sylvia Thompson, Jean and Pierre Troisgros, Jill Van Cleave, Patricia Wells, Laurie Wenk, Caroline Wheaton, Jasper White, Jonathan White, Marilyn Wilkenson, Carla Williams, Virginia Willis, John Willoughby, Deborah Winson, Lisa Yockelson.

Weldon Owen wishes to thank the following people for their generous assistance and support in producing this book: Desne Border, Ken DellaPenta, and Joan Olson.